Social Problems
and Mental Health

Social Science Lexicons

Key Topics of Study
Key Thinkers, Past and Present
Political Science and Political Theory
Methods, Ethics and Models
Social Problems and Mental Health

Social Problems and Mental Health

Edited by Jessica Kuper

ROUTLEDGE & KEGAN PAUL
LONDON AND NEW YORK

First published in 1987 by
Routledge & Kegan Paul Limited
11 New Fetter Lane, London EC4P 4EE

Published in the USA by
Routledge & Kegan Paul Inc.
in association with Methuen Inc.
29 West 35th Street, New York, NY 10001

Set in Linotron Baskerville
by Input Typesetting Ltd., London SW19 8DR
and printed in Great Britain
by Cox & Wyman Ltd,
Reading, Berks

Library of Congress Cataloging in Publication Data

Social science encyclopedia. Selections.
  Social problems and mental health.

  (Social science lexicons)
  Selections, arranged by topic, from:
The Social science encyclopedia. 1985.
  Includes bibliographies and index.
  1. Social problems—Dictionaries.   2. Mental
health—Dictionaries.   I. Kuper, Jessica.
II. Title.   III. Series.
HN13.S6524   1987   361.1'03'21   86–33878

British Library CIP Data also available
ISBN 0–7102–1170–8

Contents

Social Problems and Mental Health: the entries

abortion	loneliness
adoption	mental health
ageing	penology
alcoholism	police
alienation	pornography
anomie	poverty
anxiety	prejudice
bereavement	prostitution
capital punishment	public health
conflict, social	punishment
conflict resolution	rape
corruption	rape avoidance
crime and delinquency	rehabilitation
criminology	relative deprivation
deviance	sexual behaviour
divorce	social indicators
drug use	social welfare
ethnic groups	social welfare policy
ethnic relations	social work
gangs	stress
gerontology, social	subculture
homosexuality	suicide
incest behaviour	work and leisure
labelling theory	

Contributor List

General Editor: Jessica Kuper

Arens, William — Dept of Anthropology, State University of New York at Stonybrook

Bart, Pauline B — Dept of Psychiatry, University of Illinois at the Medical Center, Chicago

Billig, Michael — Dept of Psychology, Loughborough University

Brown, Richard K — Dept of Sociology and Social Policy, University of Durham

Calhoun, Lawrence — Dept of Psychology, University of North Carolina at Charlotte

Cann, Arnold — Dept of Psychology, University of North Carolina at Charlotte

Chambliss, William J — Dept of Sociology, University of Delaware

Cherlin, Andrew — Dept of Sociology, The Johns Hopkins University, Baltimore

Christie, Nils — Institute of Criminology and Criminal Law, University of Oslo

Cohen, G — Human Cognition Research Laboratory, Open University, Milton Keynes

Cohen, Stanley — Institute of Criminology, The Hebrew University of Jerusalem

Collard, D A — School of Humanities and Social Sciences, University of Bath

Doob, Leonard W — Dept of Psychology, Yale University

Dube-Simard, Lise — Dept of Psychology, University of Montreal

Fisher, S — University of Dundee

Glickman, Maurice — Dept of Sociology, University of Botswana

Goode, Erich	Dept of Sociology, State University of New York at Stony Brook
Gorecki, Jan	Dept of Sociology, University of Illinois at Champaign-Urbana
Hazan, Haim	Dept of Sociology and Anthropology, University of Tel-Aviv
Ingleby, David	Dept of Development Psychology, University of Utrecht
Kriesberg, Louis	Dept of Sociology, Syracuse University, Syracuse, NY
Lock, Grahame	Faculty of Social Science, Catholic University of Nijmegen, The Netherlands
Parkes, C M, MD	The London Hospital Medical College, University of London
Peplau, Anne	Dept of Psychology, University of California, Los Angeles
Pinto-Duschinsky, M	Dept of Government, Brunel University, Uxbridge, Middlesex
Plummer, K J	Dept of Sociology, University of Essex
Punch, M E	Nijenrode Business College, The Netherlands
Rock, Paul	Dept of Sociology, The London School of Economics and Political Science
Roman, Paul	Dept of Sociology, Tulane University, New Orleans
Rose, Hilary	Dept of Applied Social Studies, University of Bradford
Schur, Edwin M	Dept of Sociology, New York University
Scott, Wolf	United Nations Research Institute for Social Development, Geneva
Short, James F	Social Research Center, Washington State University, Pullman, Washington
Smooha, Sammy	Dept of Sociology, University of Haifa

Spanier, Grahame B	Provost, Oregon State University, Corvallis, Oregon
Spector, Malcolm	Dept of Sociology, McGill University, Montreal
Spielberger, Charles D	Center for Research in Behavioral Medicine and Community Psychology, University-of South Florida, Tampa, Florida
Stack, Steven	Dept of Sociology, Pennsylvania State University
Thuriaux, Michel, MD	Regional Office, World Health Organisation, Copenhagen
Timms, Noel	Dept of Social Work, University of Leicester
Tudor, Andrew	Dept of Sociology, University of York
Walker, Nigel	Institute of Criminology, University of Cambridge

Social Problems

Until the early 1970s the sociology of social problems had, for over fifty years, looked for the underlying causes of a long list of human miseries and conditions considered destructive to society and offensive to conventional morality. This field overlapped with the study of social disorganization and deviant behaviour. Since then a new set of questions has emerged giving the study of social problems a fresh start and a more independent existence. These questions began with the observation that many troublesome behaviours have, at various times, been defined in different ways. People who drink alcohol to excess were thought to be sinners by the temperance movement in the early nineteenth century, regarded as criminals by the prohibition movement in the early twentieth century and as diseased addicts by the medical establishment after 1940. Homosexuality used to be both a crime and a mental disorder. Now it is a life style, thanks to the decriminalization movement and a particularly dramatic official vote by the American Psychiatric Association in December 1973. Child battering, wife abuse, and sexual harrassment all used to be unnamed, uncounted and invisible; now they are firmly-fixed constellations in the universe of social services, official statistics and problem populations.

The new sociology of social problems attempts to describe and explain how new definitions of social problems emerge, how troublesome persons or social arrangements are identified, how institutions are created to deal with them. The field has largely abandoned the attempt to explain deviant behaviour and social disorganization. Rather, it is attempting to explain how society, through an essentially political process, discovers and invents its problems. Attention to these processes of creating meanings concerning disturbing and troublesome behaviours and conditions distinguishes the new from the old approach to social problems.

Many contemporary problems that address the inequitable treatment of racial minorities, women, children, the elderly, prisoners, mental patients, the developmentally disabled and the unborn have been put on society's agenda by the vigorous actions of social movements. Social movements have also created awareness of problems concerning pollution, toxic wastes, the dangers of nuclear energy production and the threat of nuclear holocaust.

The helping professions promote solutions to social problems and are another important participant in the social problems process. The leading examples are the medical profession and its subalterns and the social welfare bureaucracies, which together have assembled what Kittrie (1972) has termed 'the therapeutic state'. A large number of troublesome behaviours previously punished as crimes have become subject to treatment and are now considered diseases. 'Treatments' for psychopaths and sociopaths, such as lobotomies or psychosurgery, aversive conditioning and behaviour modification, electric and chemical shock have replaced more primitive societal reactions, like punishment. The objective effectiveness of these treatments is of less importance than their political appeal and the prestige of the disciplines on which they rest.

A new tradition of research on the mass media, drawing on the insights of ethnomethodology, has enlarged the study of social problems, describing the 'creation' and production of news, and explaining how systems of classification and new vocabulary both reflect and take part in the struggle to name and control controversial issues.

Governments respond to claims that define conditions as social problems by funding research on solutions to problems; establishing commissions of inquiry; passing new laws, and creating enforcement and treatment bureaucracies. But governments may also be the source of new definitions of social problems, especially embattled or ambitious agencies campaigning to increase their budgets and personnel. Research in the United States shows that the problem of marijuana use and, more recently, the concern about teenage alcoholism were created in this way.

Malcolm Spector
McGill University

Reference
Kittrie, N. (1972), *The Right to be Different*, Baltimore.

Further Reading
Conrad, P. and Schneider, J. (1980), *Deviance and Medicalization: From Badness to Sickness*, St Louis.
Spector, M. and Kitsuse, J. I. (1977), *Constructing Social Problems*, Menlo Park, Calif.
See also: *crime and delinquency; deviance; mental health.*

Abortion

The definition of induced abortion has been complicated by a debate about when 'life' can be said to begin. Frequently, however, it is defined as the intentional termination of pregnancy prior to the time at which the foetus attains viability, or capacity for life outside the womb. Cross-cultural evidence indicates that induced abortion is a universal practice (Devereux, 1955). Abortion, as a factor affecting fertility levels, has always interested demographers. The laws governing abortion at various times have reflected governmental population policies – for example, restrictions during the 1930s in the Soviet Union; encouragement of abortion in post-World War II Japan. Prior to the mid-1950s, Western social scientists other than demographers devoted little attention to the problem of abortion, although philosophers and theologians often discussed its moral implications.

Medically, the early termination of pregnancy by a trained physician under proper conditions is in most cases a simple and safe procedure. The legal status of this practice, however, has varied greatly by time and place. Since the beginning of the 1960s, the two major factors heightening social science interest in abortion are (1) concern for the possibly adverse social consequences of restrictive abortion laws; and (2) the growth and influence of the Women's Liberation Movement. Numerous studies (see Schur, 1965) have demonstrated that legal proscription does not significantly deter women from terminating unwanted pregnancies, but merely drives the demand for abortion underground, supporting an illicit market. Abortion seekers are then subject to economic and other exploitation by unscrupulous operators. The illegal operations themselves (and the attempts at self-induced abortion that typically precede them) often carry a high risk of physical as well as psychological harm.

Increasingly, abortion is recognized as a pre-eminent issue for feminists. Restrictive policies are seen to control female sexuality, impose undesired maternity, and impair women's rights to bodily self-determination. Furthermore, as Simone de Beauvoir (1953) has emphasized, abortion policies – the effects of which are felt almost entirely by women – have invariably been enacted and implemented by men (be they legislators or medical practitioners). Feminist political activity on behalf of women's reproductive rights has had a world-wide impact on public policy since the 1960s. Some of the most dramatic developments have occurred in the United States where a process of gradual legal liberalization led to a major US Supreme Court ruling (*Roe v. Wade*, 1973) legalizing abortion in the early months of pregnancy. Since that decision, there has been a sharp crystallization of 'pro-choice' (anti-restriction) and 'right to life' (pro-restriction) advocates – the latter including, but by no means limited to, Roman Catholic opponents. These groups have been actively engaged in collective organization and political action aimed at influencing public policy. Thus, in America and elsewhere the question of abortion has led to a clash of large-scale social and political movements, while the issue has continued to generate debate on a more abstract philosophical level.

Edwin M. Schur
New York University

References
Beauvoir, S. de (1953), *The Second Sex*, New York.
Devereux, G. (1955), *A Study of Abortion in Primitive Societies*, New York.
Schur, E. (1965), *Crimes Without Victims*, Englewood Cliffs, N.J.

Further Reading
Cohen, M., Nagel, T. and Scanlon, T. (eds) (1974), *The Rights and Wrongs of Abortion*, Princeton.
Jaffe, F., Lindheim, B. and Lee, P. (1981), *Abortion Politics: Private Morality and Public Policy*, New York.
Luker, K. (1975), *Taking Chances: Abortion and the Decision Not to Contracept*, Berkeley and Los Angeles.

Adoption

Adoption as an institutionalized procedure for changing a child's status has a very long, broken history. 'The ancient law books of Rome, India and Mesopotamia are full of statutes and commentaries on the subject' (Goody, 1983). Yet the first British law on adoption was only passed in 1926, after the Tomlin Report had given a cautious welcome to the idea. The ensuing years have seen an intensification of public interest in adoption, evidenced by committees of enquiry in 1954 (Hurst) and 1972 (Houghton), and by legislative changes in 1950, 1958 and 1975. During this period there have been substantial changes in the concept of adoption and in its social treatment. What was regarded in the 1920s and 1930s as a wholly unquestionable benefit for otherwise unfortunate children, bestowed through the agency of voluntary religious bodies, is now regarded less confidently and more critically in the light of changing beliefs and social forms, particularly the family.

In ancient times adoption was treated primarily as an approved method of solving heirship problems. In the present century adoption re-emerged as a provision that both benefited children and enabled couples to solve social and psychological problems consequent on their childlessness. Adoption came to be seen as a socially sanctioned, but secret, way of transferring babies from unmarried mothers to 'normal' households. The valued secrecy hid the fact of 'deviant' birth and the process of transition. Legally, the irreversible act of adoption secured definitions that emphasized the status of the child 'as if' it had been born to the adoptive parents and social arrangements underlined this.

Childless couples and others may nowadays object to any

closely drawn distinction between the purposes of adoption as serving exclusively the needs either of adults or of children. Yet adoption today is viewed increasingly as part of provision for children; their interests are treated as paramount. One illustration of this is the significant decline in the use of the adoption order in the reconstitution of families following divorce or when single mothers married for the first time. In 1974 such step-parents accounted in Great Britain for some 60 per cent (15,000) of total adoptions, but by 1982 the figure had fallen to under 6,000: the guardianship, originally proposed in the Houghton Report, became a more acceptable solution, and the Houghton arguments revolved around possible negative effects on the child of 'automatic' step-parent adoption. Another illustration of the change in orientation of the service is the growing emphasis on the adoption of children rather than infants, and on children previously considered unsuitable for adoption. In this category are to be found the physically and the mentally handicapped, black infants and black children, older children and sibling groups. As such children became a focus for adoption services, so criteria of appropriate adopters changed.

The adoption of older children in itself would make it more difficult to maintain any social fiction of the adoptee 'as if born' to the adopting parents. Other developments also encouraged the greater social visibility of adoption as such. In the 1960s a growing appreciation of the special tasks and problems of adoptive parents led to a definition of the adopting parent role as different from that of the birth parents. As people began to recognize that adoptees faced problems – this was signalled in a general but probably misleading way by a series of studies of child guidance clinic populations – support grew for the desirability of post-adoption services. By contrast, within a closed, unacknowledged view of adoption such provision is inconceivable: services are not provided simply on the basis of parenthood or childhood, so how could they be justified simply because the situation was one of adoption? Finally, as people acknowledge that 'hard to place' children have particular needs, this has led for the first time to the consideration and use of financial allowances. Symbolically, the sanctioned use of money in arrangements for adoption marks a radical change. Earlier legislation was concerned to remove any notion of financial consideration.

Questions of identity in relation to adoption have also led to legislative change and to a growing controversy concerning a particular range of adoptions, those described as transracial. Professional wisdom soon came to question the desirability of any attempt to conceal from a child his or her adoptive status, but this early stance has been elaborated. The fact of a particular status means little unless over a period of time one is given opportunities to exchange ideas about how the status came about, to give and to receive accounts of the past and one's own part in it. 'Telling' comes to be seen not as a once-for-all event; it is more a process of disclosure resulting from interaction with significant others. This kind of elaboration has been accompanied by a hesitantly accepted conviction that some minimum birth information was a matter of the adopted person's rights. Such a right was enacted in Britain in S. 26 of the Children Act, 1975, though access to birth records could not be obtained without a counselling session. Similar rights have been enacted in other countries.

The adoption of black children by white couples was initially regarded as a welcome response to disadvantage and a way of preparing the future citizens of a racially integrated society. However, earlier research on the positive results of such adoptions has been succeeded by studies which raise more questions. Perhaps the most serious criticism of transracial adoption arises from recent arguments concerning a black child's right to what is called a black identity.

Noel Timms
University of Leicester

Further Reading
Bean, P. (ed.) (1984), *Adoption: Essays in Social Policy, Law and Sociology*, London.

Goody, J. (1983), *The Development of the Family and Marriage in Europe*, Cambridge.

Haimes, E. and Timms, N. (1985), *Adoption, Identity and Social Policy*, London.

Ageing – Psychological Aspects

The study of age-related changes in cognitive processes has received fresh impetus as the proportion of elderly people in the population of Western societies continues to increase. It is important that these changes should be recognized, understood and taken into account so as to enable the elderly to cope with a modern environment and continue living a full life of work and leisure activities.

The researcher tries to isolate and identify the effects of normal ageing on cognitive abilities. Changes caused by the ageing process are confounded with associated changes in physical health, in life-style, in motivation and personality. Poor performance may be the product of sensory deficits, anxiety or lack of interest rather than mental deterioration. When old and young are compared, tests may be contaminated by cohort effects. Just as intelligence tests may be criticized for not being 'culture-fair', they can also be criticized for not being 'cohort-fair'. The educational and life experience of the generations are different and have shaped different sorts of ability. Experimental research on ageing seeks to disentangle these confounding variables and focus on the effects of age alone.

Many mental abilities do show some deterioration with age, but others are unimpaired. Individual differences tend to increase, with some individuals deteriorating while others preserve their intellect intact. In general, little decline is observable before the mid-1960s. Traditional psychometric testing has yielded age norms for performance on batteries of standard intelligence tests. The results led to a distinction between 'crystallized' (or age invariant) intelligence and 'fluid' (age sensitive) intelligence. Tests which measure intellectual attainment, such as vocabulary, verbal ability and factual knowledge, show little age effect. Tests measuring ability to manipulate or transform information such as backward digit span, or digit-symbol substitution and some tests of spatial reasoning, generally reveal a decline. These tests, however, give little insight into the changes in the underlying mechanisms that cause some abilities to be impaired and others to be preserved.

Psychologists turned, therefore, to the experimental techniques developed in the study of perception, attention, learning and memory, and applied these to the problem of ageing. The information processing approach allows complex tasks to be decomposed so that the defective component can be identified. So, for example, experimental studies of memory indicate that the process of retrieval is relatively more affected by ageing than encoding or storage (Burke and Light, 1981); and studies of mental arithmetic show that the capacity of working memory, the 'holding store', is the vulnerable component (Wright, 1981). Common factors such as a diminished rate of information processing and a diminished capacity of working memory are seen to underlie performance decrements on many tasks. The pattern of deficit can be interpreted in terms of theoretical distinctions, like that between attentional processes (ones that require conscious monitoring) and automatic processes (ones that are highly practised, rapid and unconscious). Attentional processes are more likely to be age-impaired, while automatic processes are often unaffected.

One problem that arises when complex tasks are studied is that of distinguishing between age differences in strategy and in capacity. Defective performance may result from failure to employ the right strategy rather than from reduced capacity. Where strategies are implicated, the age difference may be eliminated by remedial training. When a capacity limitation is the cause, the age difference can only be removed by restructuring the task so as to make it less demanding. The current trend in ageing research is to study performance in real-world situations with emphasis on the practical and applied aspects. For this more applied approach it is clearly very important to discover how far the difficulties old people experience in their daily lives can be overcome by training in appropriate strategies, and how far it is necessary to modify the environment to suit their capacities.

Gillian Cohen
Open University

References
Burke, D. M. and Light, L. L. (1981), 'Memory and aging: the role of retrieval processes', *Psychological Bulletin*, 90.
Wright, R. E. (1981), 'Aging, divided attention and processing capacity', *Journal of Gerontology*, 36.

Further Reading
Kausler, D. H. (1982), *Experimental Psychology and Human Aging*, New York.

See also: *gerontology*.

Alcoholism

Alcohol use has been a major social problem only since the rise of industrialized, urban societies. The likelihood that social and personal disruption will accompany drinking sharply increases in urban environments and when man–machine interaction becomes fundamental to work. At the same time, technical advances have enhanced the availability of alcoholic beverages in a wide variety of flavours, potencies and forms (Lisansky *et al.*, 1982).

Social scientists became interested in alcoholism after the repeal of Prohibition in the US in 1933. Alcoholism now came to be conceived of not as a moral failing but as a disease. This 'disease model' attributed chronic excessive drinking to a biochemical abnormality in certain individuals which created a 'craving' for alcohol once their drinking careers began (Jellinek, 1960).

Anthropologists were the first social scientists to make a significant contribution to the study of alcoholism. Documenting the variety of cultural habits related to the use of alcohol, despite the fact that it was universally known, they paved the way for the inclusion of cultural and social structural variables in the study of alcohol use and abuse (Marshall, 1980). Comparable studies of ethnic differences in alcoholism rates brought out the importance of socialization, social definition and social support (Pittman and Snyder, 1962).

Social scientists have, however, been slow to develop aetiological theories of alcohol abuse and alcoholism, and they have been impeded in part by their association with alcoholism interventionists. While this association has been the basis for the increasing commitment of public resources to alcohol-related research, most interventionists are committed to a biological aetiology of alcoholism. This is especially true of those associated with Alcoholics Anonymous. Further, the medically-oriented research establishment routinely presses for increased research allocations to studies which either directly, or by inference, propose biological solutions to alcohol problems.

There are some notable exceptions. Trice (1966) has shown that there are social personalities predisposed to alcoholism, but that their behaviour is influenced also by the 'opportunity structure' provided by drinking groups. Bacon (1973) has drawn attention to the generalized use of alcohol to facilitate social interaction. Mulford (1982) has developed a symbolic interactionist theory which focuses on the reactions of alcoholics to their social environments. Akers's (1977) social learning theory of deviant drinking combines both experiential and group-feedback elements.

Social scientists have been critical of the logic and internal consistency of the disease model of alcoholism (Calahan, 1979), and public policy has increasingly come under their scrutiny. Some of these studies have aroused considerable reaction from the North American 'alcoholism' establishment, which could affect their eventual credibility and utility.

A related body of research explores the consequences of different national and regional policies of alcohol distribution. These studies indicate that distribution policies influence the incidence of alcohol problems and alcoholism (Moore and Gerstein, 1981). Research by historians on the development of alcohol policy provides a valuable back-up to the work of the social scientists (Clark, 1976).

International comparisons have also put in question the view, common in Alcoholics Anonymous and in the treatment community, that abstinence is the only possible solution to alcohol abuse. A reduction of alcohol intake or a routinization of intake may also provide viable solutions (Heather and Robertson, 1981).

In the US, Canada and Australia, the workplace has emerged during the past decade as the primary setting within which alcoholism may be tackled. Studies are providing new insights into the processes of identifying, confronting and rehabilitating the problem drinker (Roman, 1981).

In general, then, research on alcohol abuse and alcoholism by social scientists has shifted from a primary concern with the problems of individuals and with community reaction to problem drinkers to a focus on policy and intervention. Such studies are not necessarily competitive in terms of theory or method with the claims of biomedical science.

Paul Roman
Tulane University

References

Akers, R. (1977), *Deviant Behavior and Social Learning*, Belmont, Cal.

Bacon, S. (1973), 'The process of addiction to alcohol', *Journal of Studies on Alcohol*, 34.

Calahan, D. (1970), *Problem Drinkers*, San Francisco.

Clark, N. (1976), *Deliver Us From Evil*, New York.

Heather, N. and Robertson, I. (1981), *Controlled Drinking*, London.

Jellinek, E. M. (1960), *The Disease Concept of Alcoholism*, New Haven.

Lisansky, E., White, H. and Carpenter, J. (eds) (1982), *Alcohol, Science and Society Revisited*, Ann Arbor, Mich.

Marshall, M. (ed.) (1980), *Beliefs, Behaviors, and Alcoholic Beverages*, Ann Arbor, Mich.

Moore, M. and Gerstein, G. (eds) (1981), *Alcohol and Public Policy*, Washington.

Mulford, H. A. (1982), 'The epidemiology of alcohol and its implications', in E. M. Pattison and E. Kaufman (eds), *Encyclopedic Handbook of Alcoholism*, New York.

Pittman, D. and Snyder, C. (eds) (1962), *Society, Culture and Drinking Behavior*, New York.

Roman, P. (1981), 'From employee alcoholism to employee assistance: de-emphasis on prevention and alcohol problems in work-based programs', *Journal of Studies on Alcoholism*, 42.

Trice, H. M. (1966), *Alcoholism in America*, New York.

Further Reading

Ward, D. A. (1983), *Alcoholism: An Introduction to Theory and Treatment*, Dubuque.

Alienation

Alienation (in German *Entfremdung*), sometimes called estrangement, is a psychological, sociological or philo sophical-anthropological category, largely derived from the writings of Hegel, Feuerbach and Marx.

In Hegel (1971 [1807]), we find the claim that the sphere of Spirit, at a certain stage in history, *splits up* into two regions: that of the 'actual world . . . of self-estrangement', and that of pure consciousness, which is, says Hegel, simply the 'other form' of that same estrangement. In this situation, self-consciousness is in absolute disintegration; personality is split in two. Here we have the '*entire estrangement*' of reality and thought from one another. This alienation will only be overcome when the division between Nature and Spirit is overcome – when Spirit becomes 'divested of self', that is, itself externalized.

This massive, objective, idealist philosophy of history was challenged by Feuerbach (1936[1841]) whose critique of Hegel centred precisely around a rejection of the latter's conception of the process of alienation. It is not that Feuerbach takes the 'separation' between subject and object to be a philosophical mythology. But this separation, he thinks, is assigned the status of a 'false alienation' in Hegel's work. For while man is real, God is an imaginary projection: 'the consciousness of God is the self-consciousness of man, the perception of God the self-perception of man'. Nor is nature a self-alienated form of the Absolute Spirit. But this reference to a 'false' alienation in Hegel suggests the existence of something like a 'true' – that is, really existing or operative – form of alienation. And Feuerbach does indeed believe in such a form; for it is only in some relation of contact with the objects which man produces – thus separating them off from himself – that he can become properly conscious of himself.

Marx (1975[1844]) seems to disagree. He argues that it is just by creating a world of objects through his practical activity that man proves himself as a conscious species-being. Under capitalism, however, the objects produced by human labour come to confront him as something *alien*. So the product of labour is transformed into an alien object 'exercising power over him', while the worker's activity becomes an alien activity. Marx adds that man's species-being then turns into a being alien to him, estranging him from his human aspect, and that man is thus estranged from man.

Marx's early writings, including the so-called *1844 Manuscripts*, were (re)discovered in the 1930s. Thus it was that some of their themes, including that of 'alienation', found their way into political, sociological and philosophical writings of the following period, including works of a non-Marxist character. A psychological line in alienation theory can also be identified, partially derived from Hegel (see below). The concept also, of course, has an ethical aspect: alienation is generally considered (whatever theory it derives from) a bad thing. It has even been said (Sargent, 1972) to be 'a major or even the dominant condition of contemporary life'. An abundant literature exists on recent uses of the term (see Josephson and Josephson, 1962).

Lukes (1967) has clearly identified the fundamental difference between two concepts which are apparently often confused: that of alienation, and that – introduced by Durkheim – of anomie. For Durkheim the problem of anomic man is that he needs (but misses) rules to live by, limits to his desires and to his thoughts.

Marx's problem is rather the opposite: that of man in the grip of a system from which he cannot escape.

Althusser (1969[1965]) developed a powerful critique of the notion of alienation as used by the young Marx, claiming that it was a metaphysical category abandoned by Marx in his later works.

It may finally be noted that the same term has appeared in the psychoanalytical writings of Lacan (1977[1966]), in the context of his theory of the 'mirror stage' in child development. This stage establishes an initial relation between the organism and its environment, but at the cost of a 'fragmentation' of the body. This may sound like a materialist version of Hegel's notion of the divided personality; and Lacan is indeed influenced by Hegel's analyses. It is, according to Lacan, in the relation between human subject and language that 'the most profound alienation of the subject in our scientific civilization' is to be found.

Grahame Lock
Catholic University of Nijmegen

References

Althusser, L. (1969 [1965]), *For Marx*, London. (Original French edn, *Pour Marx*, Paris.)

Feuerbach, L. (1936 [1841]), *Das Wesen des Christentums*, Berlin.

Hegel, G. W. F. (1971 [1807]), *The Phenomonology of Mind*, London. (Original German edn, *System der Wissenschaft: Erster Teil, die Phänomenologie des Geistes*, Leipzig.)

Josephson, E. and Josephson, M. (1962), *Man Alone*, New York.

Lacan, J. (1977 [1966]), *Ecrits*, London. (Original French edn, *Ecrits*, Paris.)

Lukes, S. (1967), 'Alienation and anomie', in P. Laslett and W. C. Runciman (eds), *Philosophy, Politics and Society*, Oxford.

Marx, K. (1975 [1844]), *Economic and Philosophic Manuscripts of 1844*, in K. Marx and F. Engels, *Collected Works*, vol. 3,

London. (Original German edn, *Ökonomisch-philosophische Manuskripte.*)

Sargent, L. T. (1972), *New Left Thought. An Introduction*, Homewood, Ill.

Further Reading

Blauner, R. (1964), *Alienation and Freedom. The Factory Worker and his Industry*, London.

Schaff, A. (1975), 'Alienation as a social and philosophical problem', *Social Praxis*, 3.

Sykes, G. (ed.) (1964), *Alienation. The Cultural Climate of Modern Man*, 2 vols, New York.

See also: *anomie.*

Anomie

Observations on conditions in which dominant norms are questioned or repudiated antedate Durkheim's (1947[1893]), (1951[1897]) anomie concept. Earlier writers had noted the repeated tendency of such periods to lead to diminished social cohesion (for example, Marx, 1968 [1853]) and eventually to new forms of despotism. Durkheim discerned other features: not only economic crisis but also increasing prosperity is accompanied by abeyance of established norms, that is, anomie, which releases unlimited desires and ultimately causes sharp rises in suicide rates, to an extent dependent on a nation's main religious ideology.

Widening its application to various kinds of deviance, Merton (1938) reconceptualized anomie to refer less to normlessness than to disparities between well-defined norms and limited opportunities for fulfilling them. Anomie, therefore, has two principal connotations: a weakening of rules of conduct which maintain social solidarity, and widespread frustration at the inability to achieve cultural goals. Both notions have been heavily criticized (Clinard, 1964). They are unacceptable to perspectives less concerned with emphasizing strict adherence to norms as essential to social life than with exploring how norms are manipulated, constructed, made explicit, juxtaposed, defied, and so on. Unreliability of official statistics and other difficulties in research has cast doubt on the applicability of anomie theory to suicidal behaviour and other forms of deviance. However, even stern critics, for example, Downes and Rock (1982), stop short of condemning anomie theory as otiose. It continues to command the attention of sociologists concerned with identifying sources of disenchantment with the modern world.

Maurice Glickman
University of Botswana

References

Clinard, M. (ed.) (1964), *Anomie and Deviant Behaviour*, London.

Downes, D. and Rock, P. (1982), *Understanding Deviance*, Oxford.

Durkheim, E. (1947 [1893]), *The Division of Labour in Societys*, New York. (Original French, *De la division du travail social*, Paris.)

Durkheim, E. (1951 [1897]), *Suicide*, New York. (Original French, *Le Suicide*, Paris.)

Marx, K. and Engels, F. (1968), *Selected Works*, Moscow.

Merton, R. (1938), 'Social structure and anomie', *American Sociological Review*, 3.

See also: *alienation; deviance; suicide.*

Anxiety

The term anxiety is currently used in psychology and psychiatry to refer to at least three related, yet logically different, constructs. Although most commonly used to describe an unpleasant emotional state or condition, anxiety also denotes a complex psychophysiological process that occurs as a reaction to stress. In addition, the concept of anxiety refers to relatively stable individual differences in anxiety proneness as a personality trait.

Anxiety states can be distinguished from other unpleasant emotions such as anger, sorrow or grief, by their unique combination of experiential, physiological and behavioural manifestations. An anxiety state is characterized by subjective feelings of tension, apprehension, nervousness and worry, and by activation (arousal) and discharge of the autonomic nervous system. Such states may vary in intensity and fluctuate over time as a function of the amount of stress that impinges on an individual. Calmness and serenity indicate the absence of anxiety; tension, apprehension and nervousness accompany moderate levels of anxiety; intense feelings of fear, fright and panic are indicative of very high levels of anxiety.

The physiological changes that occur in anxiety states include: increased heart rate (palpitations, tachycardia), sweating, muscular tension, irregularities in breathing (hyperventilation), dilation of the pupils, and dryness of the mouth. There may also be vertigo (dizziness), nausea, and muscular skeletal disturbances such as tremors, tics, feelings of weakness and restlessness. Individuals who experience an anxiety state can generally describe their subjective feelings, and report the intensity and duration of this unpleasant emotional reaction.

Anxiety states are evoked whenever a person perceives or interprets a particular stimulus or situation as potentially dangerous, harmful or threatening. The intensity and duration of an anxiety state will be proportional to the amount of *threat* the situation poses for the individual and the persistence of his interpretation of the situation as personally dangerous. The appraisal of a particular situation as threatening will also be influenced by the person's skills, abilities and past experience.

Anxiety states are similar to fear reactions, which are generally defined as unpleasant emotional reactions to anticipated injury or harm from some external danger. Indeed, Freud regarded fear as synonymous with 'objective anxiety', in which the intensity of the anxiety reaction was proportional to the magnitude of the external danger that evoked it: the greater the external danger, the stronger the perceived threat, the more intense the resulting anxiety reaction. Thus, fear denotes a process that involves an emotional reaction to a perceived danger, whereas the anxiety state refers more narrowly to the quality and the intensity of the emotional reaction itself.

The concept of anxiety-as-process implies a theory of anxiety as a temporally-ordered sequence of events which may be initiated by a stressful external stimulus or by an internal cue that is interpreted as dangerous or threatening. It includes the following fundamental constructs or variables: stressors, perceptions and appraisals of danger or threat, anxiety state and psychological defence mechanisms. Stressors refer to situations or stimuli that are objectively characterized by some degree of physical or psychological danger. Threat denotes an individual's subjective appraisal of a situation as potentially dangerous or harmful. Since appraisals of danger are immediately followed by an anxiety state reaction, anxiety as an emotional state is at the core of the anxiety process.

Stressful situations that are frequently encountered may lead to the development of effective coping responses that quickly eliminate or minimize the danger. However, if a person interprets a situation as dangerous or threatening and is unable to cope with the stressor, he may resort to intraphsychic manoeuvres (psychological defences) to eliminate the resulting anxiety state, or to reduce its level of intensity.

In general, psychological defence mechanisms modify, distort or render unconscious the feelings, thoughts and memories that would otherwise provoke anxiety. To the extent that a defence mechanism is successful, the circumstances that evoke the anxiety will be less threatening, and there will be a corresponding reduction in the intensity of the anxiety reaction. But defence mechanisms are almost always inefficient and often maladaptive because the underlying problems that caused the anxiety remain unchanged.

While everyone experiences anxiety states from time to time, there are substantial differences among people in the frequency and the intensity with which these states occur. Trait anxiety is the term used to describe these individual differences in the tendency to see the world as dangerous or threatening, and in the frequency that anxiety states are experienced over long periods of time. People high in trait anxiety are more vulnerable to stress, and they react to a wider range of situations as dangerous or threatening than low trait anxiety individuals. Consequently, high trait anxious people experience anxiety state reactions more frequently and often with greater intensity than do people who are low in trait anxiety.

To clarify the distinction between anxiety as a personality trait and as a transitory emotional state, consider the statement: 'Mr Smith is anxious.' This statement may be interpreted as meaning either that Smith is anxious *now*, at this very moment, or that Smith is *frequently* anxious. If Smith is 'anxious now', he is experiencing an unpleasant emotional state, which may or may not be characteristic of how he generally feels. If Smith experiences anxiety states more often than others, he may be classified as 'an anxious person', in which case his average level of state anxiety would generally be higher than that of most other people. Even though Smith may be an *anxious person*, whether or not he is *anxious now* will depend on how he interprets his present circumstances.

Two important classes of stressors have been identified that appear to have different implications for the evocation of anxiety states in people who differ in trait anxiety. Persons high in trait anxiety are more vulnerable to being evaluated by others because they lack confidence in themselves and are low in self-esteem. Situations that involve psychological threats (that is, threats to self-esteem, particularly ego-threats when personal adequacy is evaluated), appear to be more threatening for people high in trait anxiety than for low trait anxious individuals. While situations involving physical danger such as imminent surgery generally evoke high levels of state anxiety persons high or low in trait anxiety show comparable increases in anxiety state in such situations.

Individuals very high in trait anxiety, for example, psycho-neurotics or patients suffering from depression, experience high levels of state anxiety much of the time. But even they have coping skills and defences against anxiety that occasionally leave them relatively free of it. This is most likely to occur in situations where they are fully occupied with a non-threatening task on which they are doing well, and are thus distracted from the internal stimuli that otherwise constantly cue state anxiety responses.

Charles D. Spielberger
University of South Florida

Further Reading
Freud, S. (1936), *The Problem of Anxiety*, New York.
Lazarus, R. S. (1966), *Psychological Stress and the Coping Process*, New York.
Levitt, E. E. (1980), *The Psychology of Anxiety*, Hillsdale, N.J.
Spielberger, C. D. (1972), 'Anxiety as an emotional state', in C. D. Spielberger (ed.), *Anxiety: Current Trends in Theory and Research*, 2 vols, New York.
Spielberger, C. D. (1979), *Understanding Stress and Anxiety*, London.
See also: *stress*.

Bereavement

The term bereavement covers any situation in which people experience the loss of an object to which they were attached. In a narrow sense it is taken to refer to the loss by death of a loved person, but in its wider sense can cover many other losses.

Bereavement includes grief, the psychological reaction of the individual, and mourning, the social expression of grief (although this term has also been ambiguously used for the process of grieving).

Burton's claim that grief is 'the model, epitome and chief cause of melancholia' (1621) is echoed in Freud's classical paper, 'Mourning and melancholia' (1917), but it was Lindemann's study of 101 bereaved people that gave rise to the first, and arguably the best, systematic description of 'The symptomatology and management of acute grief' (1944). More recently, John Bowlby (1980) and sociologist Peter Marris (1974) have classified the nature of grief and the central place which it must play in our understanding of the human reaction to social change.

Grief is a process of psychological change through which the individual tends to pass from (1) a phase of numbness or disbelief, to (2) pining and yearning for the lost object, to (3) disorganization and despair, and followed by (4) a phase of reorganization and recovery. These phases are not clear-cut and the griever moves back and forth across them as each reminder of the loss evokes another pang of grief (Bowlby and Parkes, 1970).

During this process the individual can be seen as engaging in a struggle between competing motivations:

(a) to search for and recover the lost object;

(b) to find some way of minimizing or avoiding the pain of grief;

(c) to revise and relearn basic assumptions about the world that have been invalidated by the loss.

How these competing urges are expressed depends upon a wide range of individual and social factors, hence the confusing diversity of the manifestations of mourning reported by anthropologists (Rosenblatt *et al.*, 1976). Nevertheless, a common pattern can be discerned and has given rise to ritual observances which often seem to provide social support and a frame of reference for the bereaved, a *rite de passage*.

Because grief is so painful and because some patterns of grieving are more painful than others, it is not surprising to find that many bereaved people come to regard themselves, and to be regarded by others, as sick. While there may be some justification for regarding certain complications of grieving as pathological, the wholesale medicalization of mourning has created fresh problems for the mourner. Some bereaved people readily use alcohol or medically-prescribed drugs in order to suppress the 'symptoms' of grief and cling to mourning as a 'sick role'.

The breakdown in developed countries of extended family networks, together with disillusionment with the belief systems and loss of many of the rituals attending bereavement, has added to the plight of the bereaved, as has the increased mechanization and alienation of our systems of medical care which effectively remove the dying person from his family and deprive the family of the opportunity to care. Consequently, grief is often complicated by bewilderment, avoidance, anger and guilt.

But the pendulum is now swinging, with the emergence of hospices, bereavement counselling, self-help (or mutual help) groups and a resurgence of neighbourhood and family support for the bereaved.

Colin Murray Parkes
The London Hospital Medical School
University of London

References

Bowlby, J. (1980), *Loss: Sadness and Depression*, vol. III of *Attachment and Loss*, London.

Bowlby, J. and Parkes, C. M. (eds) (1970), 'Separation and loss', in E. J. Anthony and C. Koupernik (eds), *The Child in his Family*, vol. I, New York.

Marris, P. (1974), *Loss and Change*, London.

Rosenblatt, P. C., Walsh, R. P. and Jackson, D. A. (1976), *Grief and Mourning in Cross-Cultural Perspective*, New Haven.

Further Reading

Lindemann, E. (1944), 'The symptomatology and management of acute grief', *American Journal of Psychiatry*, 101.

Parkes, C. M. (1972), *Bereavement: Studies of Grief in Adult Life*, London.

Capital Punishment

Capital punishment is an historical condition. Accompanied by torture, it is widely applied and taken for granted in primitive societies, past and present (see, for example, Diamond, 1971). Cultural progress brings a tendency toward decreasing severity of criminal punishments, and, especially, toward decreasing use of the death penalty (Gorecki, 1983). This pattern has been particularly marked in European history; however, the total abolition of capital punishment only became a publicly articulated demand after the Enlightenment. Today, most liberal democracies do not have the death penalty. The United States is the most conspicuous exception. Following a protracted struggle which they very nearly lost, the American retentionists won, by a crucial Supreme Court decision of 1976; thus a number of the states in the US continue to punish the most abominable cases of murder by death. This development was precipitated by the increasing public anger against high crime rates in America. On the other hand, many authoritarian, especially totalitarian, societies apply capital punishment profusely; in those societies the will of the despots affects criminal law, and the despots are rarely open to abolitionist arguments.

The arguments of both abolitionists and retentionists are many and hotly debated. The most forcefully stressed retentionist plea is utilitarian (or, strictly speaking, teleological): capital punishment is claimed to deter wrongdoing even better than lifelong confinement. There are further utilitarian contentions as well – that capital punishment constitutes the only secure incapacitation, and that it increases respect for criminal law. Non-utilitarian retentionists believe in the ultimate retributive value of capital punishment as the only 'just desert' for the most abhorrent crimes. In rejoinder, the abolitionists question the superior deterrent value of the death penalty. Furthermore, they stress the sanctity of human life and immorality of the state killing anyone. They argue that the penalty brutalizes society, that it is inevitably arbitrarily imposed, and that it endangers the innocent, since judicial errors do occur. They feel that the suffering of convicts led to execution and of those who wait on death row are appalling. Many believe in the re-education of wrongdoers rather than in retribution as the basic goal of criminal justice, and complain that execution is both vindictive and precludes rehabilitation.

The logical status and empirical validity of these arguments vary. The non-utilitarian arguments constitute moral axioms, like any ultimate ethical norms. On the other hand, the utilitarian arguments are questionable on purely empirical grounds. This is particularly true of the deterrence idea, which has stimulated a wealth of statistical inquiries aimed at its testing. Despite their increasing refinement (especially by Ehrlich, 1975, and his opponents), the inquiries have been inconclusive; we do not know and may never learn whether capital punishment deters most effectively.

With the impact of the death penalty on effective functioning of criminal justice unproved and uncertain, the heat of the capital punishment debate seems hardly justified by practical needs. On the other hand, whether we send criminals to their death presents a moral dilemma of the utmost importance. That is why interest in the issue remains intense, especially in societies which have not yet opted for abolition.

Jan Gorecki
University of Illinois
Champaign-Urbana

References
Diamond, A. S. (1971), *Primitive Law Past and Present*, London.
Ehrlich, I. (1975), 'The deterrent effect of capital punishment: a question of life and death', *American Economic Review*, 65.
Gorecki, J. (1983), *Capital Punishment – Criminal Law and Social Evolution*, New York.
See also: *penology; punishment.*

Conflict, Social

Social scientists are interested in two aspects of conflict: how conflict relations permeate and shape all aspects of human interaction and social structure (that is, a conflict perspective to social life), and how a conflict or other theoretical perspective helps elucidate the genesis, escalation, de-escalation, and outcome and consequences of wars, revolutions, strikes and uprisings.

Conflict Perspective
Stated at a necessarily high level of generality, writers using the conflict approach (as opposed to, say, a functionalist, exchange, or systems approach) seek to explain not only how social order is maintained, but how it is maintained despite great inequalities, and also how social structures change. They view societies, organizations and other social systems as arenas for

personal or group contests. (Complementary and common interests are not excluded, but the competitive and incompatible character of interests are emphasized.) Coercion is a major way in which people seek to advance their interests. It is assumed that humans generally do not want to be dominated or coerced, and therefore resist attempts at coercion, and struggles ensue.

Conflict theory has a long tradition going back to the beginnings of cynical counsel to rulers and naturalistic history, as can be seen in the writings of Thucydides, Machiavelli and Hobbes. Marx stressed the material conditions underlying conflict, especially class struggles based upon property relations. Other conflict theorists such as Gumplowitz, Ratzenhofer and Novicow worked in the context of evolutionary thought and posited a group struggle for existence; they variously stressed military power in conflict, and interests – for example, ethnic differences – as bases for conquest. Simmel was another classical sociologist concerned with the forms and consequences of conflict.

Interest in the conflict perspective revived, at least in English-speaking countries, in the 1960s. In preceding decades the dominant social-science theories portrayed societies as based on consensus and consent, but the political turmoil of the sixties, both domestic and international, directed attention to social conflicts and to the conflict approach.

Recent conflict theorists have emphasized different combinations of elements from the rich conflict tradition. Many contemporary social scientists regard themselves as Marxists, but they differ a great deal in their interpretations of Marx and in the way they have developed elements of dialectical materialism in analysing contemporary social life. Some stress the clash of immediate economic interests, others the divisions based on ideological structures, while still others focus on the role of nonclass divisions such as ethnicity and sex in shaping conflicts. Many conflict theorists stress their differences with Marxism, or they simply emphasize certain factors and processes which Marxists do not. The work of Dahrendorf (1959) and Collins (1975) are illustrative. Dahrendorf argued that authority relations, not property relations, underlie social conflict. Collins considered coercion, including violence, as important means of control, and he drew from the symbolic-interaction tradition to stress the importance of meanings in the organization of people for struggle, both at the interpersonal and the social-structural levels.

The study of economic development provides one example of how the conflict perspective has become important in all branches of the social sciences, and in many topics of inquiry. The conflict approach in this context stresses the use of power (economic, political and military) to impose unequal exchanges which lead to a world-system marked by dependency; several economists and sociologists have sought to account for under-development in the Third World using this perspective.

Social Conflicts
Social scientists have recently looked for a comprehensive explanation of all social conflicts, for, despite their differences, they all have important similarities:
(1) As a form of social interaction, adversary groups, or persons purporting to represent contending groups, take each other into account in waging the conflict.
(2) Collectivities based upon social categories and divisions develop a sense of group consciousness partly out of their antagonistic interaction with each other.
(3) The adversaries believe that what each seeks from the other is at least partly incompatible.
(4) The interacting parties engage in a series of exchanges or encounters, so that we can recognize a struggle with a course of development.

Types of Social Conflict
Variations in types of social conflicts affect the way they emerge, escalate, and de-escalate. Among the many variations are three particularly significant and interrelated factors: the character of the parties, the nature of the goals, and the means used in the struggle.
(1) Conflicting parties differ in their degree of organization and boundedness. At one extreme are governments, trade

unions and other entities with membership rules and generally recognized roles for forming and executing policy towards adversaries. At the other extreme are more nebulous entities such as social classes and believers in a common ideology where boundaries of adherence may be disputed or in flux, and which generally lack recognized roles for contending with adversaries. Moreover, every social conflict is likely to include many sets of adversaries; some overlap and cross-cut, or one encompasses some entities and is encompassed by others. For example, heads of governments may claim to speak for a government, a state, a people, an ideology, a political party faction, and a social class. Each such claim helps constitute a corresponding adversary. Herein lies one of the bases for the interlocking character of conflict.

(2) Social conflicts are about incompatible goals, and the nature of these goals are another basis for distinguishing different kinds of conflicts. Adversaries may contest control over land, money, or other resources which they all value: such disputes over resources are *consensual* conflicts. Alternatively they may come into conflict about differently held values, for example, ideology or religion. These are *dissensual* conflicts. Of course, in specific conflicts both consensual and dissensual components are likely to be present. In addition, goals differ in the degree to which the adversaries consider the issue in contention to be important or even vital.

(3) Conflicts are waged in a variety of ways. Conflict analysts are particularly interested in struggles involving great coercion, whether employed or threatened, and coercion which is relatively uninstitutionalized. In many conflicts, the adversaries adhere to well-developed and highly-institutionalized rules; indeed, these are often not regarded as social conflicts at all. This may be the case, for instance, in electoral campaigns, where different parties seek to control the government. Certain kinds of conflicts may become increasingly institutionalized and regulated over time, and that transformation is a matter of paramount significance. We can recognize such a change in labour-management conflicts in many countries during the nineteenth century (Dahrendorf, 1959).

Aside from the theoretical issues, the value orientations of the investigators are also crucial in the study of conflicts. Some tend to approach social conflict from a partisan perspective, trying to learn how to advance the particular goals of their side. This is the case for military strategists and many advocates of national liberation. Others are concerned to minimize violence and look for alternative ways of defending or attaining sought-for goals. Still others are primarily interested in attaining a new social order, justified in terms of universal claims for justice or equity; they may see conflicts as the natural process towards this end. Finally, the intellectually curious adopt a disinterested, relativistic view of social conflicts.

Origins of Social Conflict
Social scientists mostly look for the origins of social conflicts in social, political and economic relations and do not reduce them to the innate biological nature of humans. (Such factors seem inadequate to explain the variations in conflicts.) But conditions and processes internal to one party in a conflict may be stressed in accounting for a fight or for the means used in waging the struggle. For example, resentments arising from dissatisfaction from one source may be displaced upon easily targeted scapegoats. This produces an unrealistic conflict, in the sense that it is not based on any objective condition, or that the means employed are disproportionate to the issues at stake. It is difficult to assess the objective basis and appropriate means for solving a conflict, although recent work is contributing something in this direction, as noted below.

Most conflict theorists stress inequality as the underlying basis for conflict: if it appears to one party that the other is gaining at their expense, this is the basis for consensual conflict. Other conflicts may relate to disagreements about desired goals – when groups have different values and wish to impose their own upon the other, the objective conditions for a dissensual conflict exist. Functionalist theorists emphasize the dissensual bases of social conflicts, particularly dissensus resulting from unequal rates of social change in the social system. Concentrating on the functional integration and consensual character of social systems, they tend to view conflicts as flowing from their disruption (Johnson, 1966). This focus helps to account for behaviour which analysts regard as expressive rather than instrumental.

Awareness by adversaries that they are in conflict is necessary for a conflict to exist – analysts do not agree about how such awareness comes about. Some argue that absolute deprivation is a major factor, while others regard relative deprivation as more important – that is, how deprived people feel compared to their expectations based on past experience, or relative to comparative groups (Gurr, 1970). In any event, the group members' beliefs that they are able to improve their conditions are crucial, and these beliefs vary with developments in each contesting party and in their relations with each other. Groups must also be able to mobilize to pursue their goals (Tilly, 1978). Pre-existing linkages of persons and groups help to channel mobilization, while leadership and the shared ideologies of possible recruits are also key factors.

The fact that relatively dominant groups are able to attain their goals helps to explain why they may initiate further demands leading to overt conflict. And if the subordinate group should believe that they can effectively challenge the status quo, the dominant group may react by attempting to meet the challenge and by persuading others to regard the status quo as legitimate.

Conflict Management
Most studies of social conflicts have focused on the emergence of conflict behaviour and its escalation, but recently there is greater interest shown in de-escalation and conflict management. The means used in waging a conflict can vary greatly in intensity and extent. Inducements in a conflict are also noncoercive. While coercion encompasses a variety of violent and nonviolent means, noncoercion includes efforts at persuasion and positive sanctions, such as promised benefits (Kriesberg, 1982; Ebert, 1981). Escalation and de-escalation are affected by (1) the internal developments in each of the adversary

groups; (2) the interaction between them, and (3) the conduct of actors not initially involved in the conflict.

(1) Internal factors include various social-psychological processes and organizational developments which lead to an increasing commitment to the cause of the struggle. Sub-units engaged in the conflict may derive power, status and economic gains by building up their fighting resources (Senghaas, 1972), while those who suffer in the struggle, especially if they are much more severely affected than their adversaries, may become less committed.

(2) The manner in which the two sides interact is significant: adversary actions can be strong, provocative and escalating, or successfully intimidating and de-escalating; or the actions can be conciliatory and thus de-escalating, or appeasing and thereby encouraging escalation. Evidence suggests that if both sides are more or less equally antagonistic, then the conflict is less likely to escalate.

(3) Parties not initially involved in the conflict can affect the course of conflict by joining in later in order to advance their own interests, or by setting limits to the conflict. Intermediaries can also mitigate the undesired aspects of conflicts by mediation, thus facilitating communication and providing face-saving options.

Adversaries in conflicts generally evaluate the outcomes in terms of victories and defeats, wins or losses. In addition, there are possible mutual losses and gains because of the interlocking character of conflicts. Functionalists will examine the functions of social conflicts for the parties and the larger system in which the conflicts occur. But analysts adopting a conflict perspective are also likely to observe that not only are conflicts endemic, but they are ways of bringing about needed changes.

Louis Kriesberg
Syracuse University

References

Collins, R. (1975), *Conflict Sociology*, New York.

Dahrendorf, R. (1959), *Class and Class Conflict in Industrial Society*, London.

Ebert, T. (1981), *Gewaltfreier Aufstand*, Waldkirch.

Gurr, T. R. (1970), *Why Men Rebel*, Princeton, N.J.

Johnson, C. (1966), *Revolutionary Change*, Boston.

Kriesberg, L. (1982), *Social Conflicts* (2nd edn), Greenwich, Conn.

Senghaas, D. (1972), *Rüstung und Militarismus*, Frankfurt/Main.

Tilly, C. (1978), *From Mobilization to Revolution*, Reading, Mass.

Further Reading

Boulding, K. E. (1962), *Conflict and Defense*, New York.

Burton, J. W. (1969), *Conflict and Communication: The Use of Controlled Communication in International Relations*, London.

Galtung, J. (1980), *The True Worlds: A Transnational Perspective*, New York.

Schelling, T. C. (1980), *The Strategy of Conflict*, Cambridge, Mass.

See also: *conflict resolution*.

Conflict Resolution

Conflicts are inevitable because resources and time are limited or because alternative courses of action are usually numerous. The individual, acting by himself, decides to express or repress an impulse. Together with other persons in a group, he competes with another group to capture honours or to improve a common status. As a member of a tribe, an ethnic grouping, or a nation, he and his compatriots believe they are compelled to struggle with a rival or enemy to secure or maintain what they consider to be their sovereign or justifiable rights. Undoubtedly some conflicts are desirable: the spice they add to living provides an incentive to achieve personal or group goals (Coser, 1956). But many, perhaps most, conflicts are painful or non-productive; hence conflict resolutions are consciously or unconsciously, whole- or halfheartedly pursued.

If there were a magic formula or procedure for resolving conflicts, as there is not, modern societies would have, for example, fewer psychiatric institutes, riots, and wars.

To simplify the present exposition, a value judgement is explicitly made: a person or some persons in conflict seek a 'favourable' resolution. Conflicts are assumed to be resolvable – if a hedge be tolerated – at least in the long run. Resolutions result either from an external constraint or from a somewhat prolonged interaction between competing impulses or individuals. In the first category would be a person who, wishing to be counter-aggressive toward an insulting stranger, curbs his hostility in accordance with a rigid convention in that social situation; representatives of management and labour who have agreed to submit disputes to binding arbitration; or a small, relatively powerless country like Belgium which could not repel invading German armies in both World Wars. We consider here interactions leading or not leading to challenging resolutions: the smoker cannot resist the urge to smoke, but would avoid lung damage; workers strike and the plant shuts down; two great powers idiotically strengthen their nuclear arsenals.

Apparently intractable conflicts may be resolvable when and if it is possible to peer beneath the ostensible reasons for their existence and thus to uncover the 'real' objectives. A conflict betwen two persons seeking an advantage only one of them can attain may lead to a compromise or a zero-sum solution with a winner and a loser. The verbal, emotional phrasing of demands, however, does not necessarily reflect 'real' desires which, if ascertainable, could be integrated into a creative resolution. For a holiday a wife would go to Place A, her husband to Place B; after coolly determining the underlying goal of each, they select Place C which provides the wife with the natural beauty she seeks and the husband with the sports attainable at B. This oversimplified, hypothetical analogy may indeed function as a guiding model to creative resolutions of conflict, in spite of the sceptical assertion that only a compromise has been achieved, since Place C may not be as satisfying as A would have been to the wife and B to the husband.

In real life and in the absence of external constraints, therefore, three sometimes insuperable difficulties must be overcome to achieve a resolution of a conflict:

(1) The party or parties must seek a resolution and be willing and able to interact within himself or with others. The disturbed person who cannot decide whether to be or not to be faces the cosmic or trivial alternatives, or seeks aid from a friend, clergyman, or psychiatrist. Contending parties in an industrial or international dispute agree to negotiate or refer their differences to a third party such as an arbitration board, a court, or the United Nations Security Council. Traditional societies have often evolved standardized procedures to resolve internal disputes (Gulliver, 1979).

(2) Problems that can plague interactions are legion. In psychoanalysis and some other non-physiological therapies, the patients' repressed or significant impulses do not readily emerge from their unconscious or unverbalizable cages; or relevant behaviour modification is elusive. During negotiations the parties in conflict are likely to mistrust each other and quite naturally seek to win as many concessions as possible from an opponent, evidence for which abounds and is ever discoverable at every international confrontation especially, to our sorrow, in modern times. As each party caucuses before and during the negotiation, its members who are not supermen are prone to exhibit all imaginable human frailties: misperceptions, projections upon others, stereotypes, defective information, selective exposure, exaggerated vigilance, defensive avoidance, impatience, feigned conformity in the interest of in-group morale, in fact all the shortcomings that make ordinary and extraordinary decision making considerably less rational than some classical economists, theoretical political scientists, and logicians perforce assume (Janis, 1982; Jervis, 1976).

On the basis of well-controlled experiments with atypical subjects under artificial conditions (Abelson and Levi, 1983; Collins and Guetzkow, 1964), of conferences or workshops arranged by private organizations such as Friends and Pugwash (Doob, 1975), of labour-management confrontations (Vroom and Yetton, 1973), and a pathetically small number of international meetings employing the non-shuttle diplomacy of Trieste (Campbell, 1976) and Camp David, a dash of optimism can be injected into comtemporary gloom. Under specified conditions conflicts can be creatively resolved to the satisfaction of all parties, or at least progress toward that end is possible. Non-neurotic persons of good will, capable of participating and striving to reach a novel resolution, assemble for some period of time, probably many days or weeks, at a neutral site where they feel detached and comfortable. Mass media are excluded. Under the auspices of a third party, whether an arbitrator, intervener, or mediator, the participants are taught to recognize their own psychological and social strengths and weaknesses and to improve the ways in which they communicate with others. Preaching and lecturing are not likely to be efficacious; instead new insights and methods are actually experienced both intellectually and emotionally (Burton, 1969). The phrasing of propositions (Fisher and Ury, 1981); the subtle use of experiential devices like simulation (direct or reverse role-playing); and the implementation of deliberate training programmes such as those provided by T-Groups (Bradford, Gibb, and Benne, 1964), Tavistock (Miller and Rice, 1967), and other practitioners (e.g., Delbecq, Van de Ven, and Gustafson, 1975) facilitate understanding and promote the kind of consensus contributing to a conflict's resolution.

(3) These obstacles appear after the participants leave the intimate, face-to-face situation and re-enter their normal milieu. Even if they themselves are important policy-makers, they must convince their followers' that the achieved resolution is desirable; or as official or unofficial representatives they must effectively communicate that resolution to their superiors. They may have grown to love one another and their opponents while momentarily detached from the conflict, but now they face suspicion and hostility from non-participants. Unanticipated changes in conditions may occur. The resolution realized at a distance, in short, may turn out to be unrealizable in the workaday arena (Doob and Foltz, 1974). On the other hand, the transition from dreams to reality need not always be tortuous

or impossible. Perhaps the basis for a resolution at a more opportune time in the future may have been created.

Leonard W. Doob
Yale University

References

Abelson, R. P. and Levi, A. (1983), 'Decision-making and decision theory', in G. Lindzey and E. Aronson (eds), *Handbook of Social Psychology* (3rd edn), Reading, Mass.

Bradford, L. P., Gibb, J. R. and Benne, K. (1964), *T-Group Theory and Laboratory Method*, New York.

Burton, J. (1969), *Conflict and Communication*, London.

Campbell, J. C. (ed.) (1976), *Successful Negotiation: Trieste, 1954*, Princeton.

Collins, B. E. and Guetzkow, H. (1964), *A Social Psychology of Group Processes for Decision-Making*, New York.

Coser, L. (1956), *The Functions of Social Conflict*, New York.

Delbecq, A. A., Van de Ven, A. H. and Gustafson, D. H. (1975), *Group Techniques for Program Planning*, Glenview, Ill.

Doob, L. W. (1975), 'Unofficial intervention in destructive social conflicts', in R. W. Brislin, S. Bochner, and W. J. Lonner (eds), *Cross-Cultural Perspectives on Learning*, New York.

Doob, L. W. and Foltz, W. J. (1974), 'The impact of a workshop upon grass-roots leaders in Belfast', *Journal of Conflict Resolution*, 18.

Fisher, R. and Ury, W. (1981), *Getting to Yes*, Boston.

Gulliver, P. H. (1979), *Disputes and Negotiations*, New York.

Janis, I. L. (1982), *Groupthink* (2nd edn), Boston.

Jervis, R. (1976), *Perception and Misperception in International Politics*, Princeton.

Miller, E. J. and Rice, A. K. (1967), *Systems of Organization*, London.

Vroom, V. H. and Yetton, P. W. (1973), *Leadership and Decision Making*, Pittsburgh.

See also: *conflict*.

Corruption

In its most general sense, corruption means the perversion or abandonment of a standard. Hence it is common to speak of the corruption of language or of moral corruption. More narrowly, corruption refers to the abandonment of expected standards of behaviour by those in authority for the sake of unsanctioned personal advantage. In the business sphere, a company director is deemed corrupt if he sells his private property to the company at an inflated price, at the expense of the shareholders whose interests he is supposed to safeguard. Lawyers, architects and other professionals are similarly guilty of corruption if they take advantage of their clients to make undue personal gains.

Political corruption can be defined as the misuse of public office or authority for unsanctioned private gain. Several points about the definition should be noted. (1) Not all forms of misconduct or abuse of office constitute corruption. An official or a government minister who is merely incompetent or who betrays government secrets to a foreign power for ideological reasons is not generally considered corrupt. (2) Legislators and public officials in most countries are entitled to salaries and other allowances. Corruption occurs only when they receive additional *unsanctioned* benefits, such as bribes. In practice, it is frequently hard to draw the line between authorized and unauthorized payments and, in any case, this will change over time and will be drawn differently in different countries. A benefit regarded as a bribe in one country may be seen as normal and legitimate in another. Legal definitions of corrupt practices are only an imperfect guide since benefits forbidden by law are often sanctioned by social custom, and vice versa. The boundaries of accepted behaviour can be especially difficult to determine in countries affected by rapid political and social change. (3) *Electoral corruption* needs to be defined differently from other forms. Whereas most political corruption involves the abuse of public office, electoral corruption is the abuse of the process by which public office is won.

Common forms of corruption are bribery, extortion (the unauthorized extraction of money by officials from members of the public) and misuse of official information. Bribery need not consist of a direct payment to a public official. 'Indirect bribery' may take the form of a promise of a post-retirement job, the provision of reduced-price goods, or the channelling of business to a legislator or to members of his family.

Corruption was a serious problem in biblical and classical times, and was found in most periods of history. Cases of judicial corruption were particularly frequent. By the 1960s, an influential school of 'revisionist' political scientists nevertheless presented an optimistic view about the decline of corruption in advanced Western democracies (see Heidenheimer, 1970). Some of the 'revisionists' maintained that corruption did not present as grave a problem as previous writers had suggested. In many newly independent nations, where corruption was supposedly rampant, the practices condemned by Western observers as corrupt (for example, making payments to low-level officials for routine services) were accepted as normal by local standards. Moreover, some forms of corruption, far from damaging the process of social and economic development, could be positively beneficial. Bribery enabled entrepreneurs (including foreign companies) to cut through red tape, thereby promoting the economic advance of poor nations. Corruption was seen as a transitory phenomenon, which was likely to decline as economic and social progress was achieved. The general trend was to be seen, it was argued, in the history of Britain and the United States. In Britain, electoral corruption, the sale of titles and government jobs, and corruption relating to public contracts had been rife until the nineteenth century. The introduction of merit systems of appointment to the civil service, the successful battle against electoral corruption and a change in public attitudes towards the conduct of government had led to a dramatic decline in corruption – a decline which coincided with the nation's economic development. Similarly, in the United States, corruption had been rampant in the late nineteenth and early twentieth centuries. This had been a period of intense economic and social change. As suggested by Robert Merton, the corrupt urban party machines, such as the Democratic Party organization in New York City (Tammany Hall) had provided avenues for advancement for underprivileged immigrant groups. After the Second World War, full employment, the advance of education, the decline of political patronage and the growth of public welfare benefits combined to eliminate the deprivation that had previously led to corruption. A new civic culture replaced the former loyalties to family and to ethnic group. According to a common view, the party machine and the corruption that had accompanied it withered away.

This interpretation has recently come under challenge. Corruption is neither so benign in underdeveloped countries, nor is it so rare in advanced ones as previously thought. It is unrealistic to suppose that advances in education or in techniques of public administration, the development of a 'public-regarding ethos' or economic development can lead to the virtual disappearance of corruption. The growth of governmental activity and regulation in the modern state increases the opportunities and the temptations for corruption. Improvements in education need not lead to the elimination of corruption but to its perpetuation in new, sophisticated forms.

Revelations since the 1970s have led scholars to give increased attention to the contemporary problems of corruption in advanced democracies and in communist countries. In the United States, the Watergate affair of 1972–4 led to a wave of investigations that resulted in hundreds of convictions for corruption, including that of Vice-President Spiro Agnew. Others convicted included the governors of Illinois, Maryland, Oklahoma and West Virginia. Rampant corruption was uncovered in a number of states including Florida, New Jersey, Pennsylvania and Texas. In Britain, the conventional view about the virtual elimination of corruption was shattered by several major scandals in the 1970s. The far-reaching Poulson scandal, involving local government corruption in the north of England as well as members of Parliament, erupted in 1972. Local government corruption was proved in South Wales, Birmingham and in Scotland, while in London senior police officers were imprisoned. Japan, Italy and Israel are among other economically developed coutries where there have been recent revelations about corruption. In the communist sphere, there have been academic studies as well as official campaigns against corruption in the Soviet Union, China and Poland. The wide scope of governmental activity and control in these countries leads to a correspondingly wide scope for practices to evade this control. Forms of corruption that have been the focus of attention in a number of countries include police corruption and bribery involving multinational corporations (for example, in the arms trade).

The definition, causes and effects of corruption and techniques of reform continue to be matters of controversy among sociologists and political scientists. What has been established beyond dispute is that political corruption is a widespread, pervasive and potentially serious phenomenon.

M. Pinto-Duschinsky
Brunel University, Uxbridge

References
Clarke, M. (ed.) (1983), *Corruption: Causes, Consequences and Control*, London.
Heidenheimer, A. J. (ed.) (1970), *Political Corruption: Readings in Comparative Analysis*, New York.

Crime and Delinquency

The study of crime and delinquency is an interdisciplinary inquiry which brings together the theoretical and methodological insights of sociology, economics, political science, psychology and law. The field consists of two interrelated but separable areas of concern: the development and implementation of laws which define acts and people as criminal or delinquent, and the social, psychological and biological forces that cause people to commit acts of crime and delinquency.

Much of the work of social scientists studying crime and delinquency leads to the debunking of commonplace myths. For example, historical research on the process whereby acts come to be defined as crime (murder, theft, vagrancy, assault, and so on) contradicts the commonsensical view that the customary beliefs of the people or a society's 'moral consensus' determines which acts are defined as criminal. Most acts are defined as criminal precisely because there is little consensus that they should be. It is the political struggles taking place at the time that culminate in one interest group succeeding in getting their ideas enshrined in law. Thus, murder was defined as an offence against the state in early England in the Crown's struggle against the power of the Church and the feudal aristocracy; by removing their control over disputes amongst the citizens, the Crown greatly enhanced its power. The theft of wood, killing of game and poaching of fish from 'common grounds' was incorporated into the criminal law and deemed so serious that violators could be put to death, at a time when the Crown sought to reward loyal nobles by giving them private hunting and fishing grounds.

In a field as diverse and politically sensitive as the study of crime and delinquency, there are few incontrovertible facts and theories. High on the list of accepted truths, however, is the fact that in most societies people in all social classes and in all groups commit crimes at some time in their lives. Thus a theory of why people commit crimes must account for what is defined in law as criminal or delinquent but what is in fact normal, in the sense of being almost universal amongst the population. A further fact generally agreed upon is that while everyone commits some acts of crime in almost every society, the age from fifteen to twenty-five is the period in life when people are most apt to engage in delinquent and criminal acts. Indeed, even people who engage in some types of crime with regularity during this age period tend to stop committing criminal acts after the age of twenty-five.

It is also clear that the definition of acts and actors as criminal, as well as the way crime is depicted in a society, are politically determined events. For example, officially published crime rates in most countries of the world show a marked increase in the incidence of criminal and delinquent behaviour in the past century. Criminologists have been sceptical about these statistics, since a decision to report an incident as a crime is a bureaucratic one which is heavily influenced in every country by the politics of crime reporting.

Police departments and governments manipulate statistics to serve the interests of the bureaucracy and the political desires of the government. Furthermore, the way in which the statistics are gathered, even when they are not intentionally manipulated, renders them useless as an index of the amount and type of crime taking place. Crimes of the upper classes are rarely represented by official statistics, and crimes of the lower classes are usually exaggerated in the direction of appearing much more serious than they in fact are (Chambliss and Seidman, 1971). Criminologists therefore rely more heavily on carefully conducted research for a picture of the quality and quantity of crime than they do on official statistics. In recent years population surveys asking whether a person has been the victim of a crime provide a better, although far from perfect, picture of the incidence and distribution of crime. But even these surveys tend to be biased by not including categories of crime typical of upper class and business criminality.

The enforcement of criminal law reflects the class system of the society. In Western capitalist democratic societies the enforcement of criminal laws against the upper classes for business crimes and political corruption are rare in comparison with the enforcement of criminal laws against minor offences of the lower classes such as gambling, drug taking, vagrancy and being disorderly in public. In every Western society most of the arrests (usually over 80 per cent) made every year by the police are of lower class persons accused of committing minor offences. The arrest rate for more serious offences, whether committed by lower, middle or upper class persons, is quite low.

In the history of the study of crime and delinquency, four overarching, general paradigms have dominated research and theory: (1) the social psychological, (2) sociological, (3) biological and (4) Marxian.

(1) The social psychologists see crime and delinquency as emanating from the life experiences of individuals. There are many different theories in this tradition including (a) the psychoanalytic theory which stresses the importance of family relations and interpersonal conflicts as the source of criminal or delinquent actions; (b) the cultural approach which postu-

lates the existence of criminal and delinquent subcultures which are learned by some people in the same fashion that non-criminal actions are learned by others; (c) the 'societal reaction' or 'labelling' approach which postulates that people become delinquent because they are caught and labelled by parents, peers, teachers or police; and (d) the anomie theory that argues that it is a failure of some people to internalize consensually held norms that leads them to be delinquent or criminal.

(2) Although biological theories have largely been in disrepute since the 1900s, there has been a resurgence of interest in these theories in the last few years. In general they argue that a certain combination of genetic and biological predispositions increases the likelihood that delinquent acts will occur if social and personal experiences are such as to exacerbate these tendencies.

(3) The sociological tradition focuses on different propensities towards crime by people located in different social classes in the society. Opinions differ, however, about what characteristics of social class are most fundamental in determining the likelihood that people will commit crime. Some sociologists argue that the cause of crime is cultural, and therefore social class membership makes it more likely that people will learn criminal behaviour from people who value crime as a way of life (Sutherland and Cressey, 1984). Other sociologists argue that social class restricts opportunities for success and therefore some members will possibly resort to crime as an alternative means of achieving success. Most sociologists agree that social class is a starting point for an understanding of crime. People in the upper, middle and lower classes commit crimes that are a reflection of their class position; this does not mean that crime is necessarily limited to those in the lower classes.

(4) The Marxian tradition accepts the legitimacy of the sociological emphasis on social class but argues that crime is a reflection of structural contradictions in the political economy and class struggle. There are several theoretical traditions within the Marxian framework; especially important are the instrumentalist and dialectical theories. (a) The instrumentalist theory argues that the ruling class defines lower class behav-

iours as criminal in an effort to maintain control over them; the lower classes protest against ruling class control by committing criminal acts. (b) A more sophisticated Marxian approach involves the idea that the contradictions of a period's political and economic systems generates pressure towards criminal behaviour on members of different social classes. The capitalist class resorts to crime in an effort to maintain and enhance the accumulation of capital, where illegal means are more effective than legal ones (the conspiring to restrain trade, engaging in the importation and distribution of illegal commodities such as drugs, etc). The lower class resorts to crime so that they are able to purchase the commodities which they, along with everyone else, are encouraged to want in a system that depends on commodity consumption for its economic survival.

Criminologists believe that research and critical appraisal will resolve these differences of theory. The faith is, alas, not based on past experience. Yet, there are certain facts which any theory must fit, and it is a failure to meet this criteria which renders many of the existing traditions untenable. For example, it is well established that in the course of a lifetime *most* people – probably almost 100 per cent – commit a large number of criminal acts. Any theory that postulates some unique set of social, personal or biological experiences differentiating criminals from non-criminals is therefore suspect. If everyone commits crime, then it is nonsense to suppose that we can explain why some people commit crime while others do not. Thus theories of crime that do no recognize the universality of criminal behaviour are necessarily faulted from the start.

Connected to this observation is the fact that even if one limits the problem of explanation to those who commit 'serious' crimes or those whose criminality is ongoing and part of a 'way of life', there is the second pillar of established fact: both the upper and lower classes produce large numbers of people in both of these categories. Thus any theory that argues for differences in the seriousness or incidence of crime as a result of differences in social class position must also be wanting. The modern world institutionalized the use of illegal means by one government to overthrow unfriendly political forces in another, including assassination and illegal supplying of military equipment. These and other crimes of the powerful are fundamental facts which any explanation of crime must fit.

William J. Chambliss
University of Delaware

References
Chambliss, W. J. and Seidman, R. B. (1971), *Law, Order and Power*, Reading, Mass.
Sutherland, E. H. and Cressey, D. R. (1984), *Principles of Criminology*, Philadelphia.

Further Reading·
Chambliss, W. J. (1984), *Criminal Law in Action*, New York.
Christie, N. (1981), *The Limits of Pain*, Oxford.
Clinard, M. B. and Yeager, P. C. (1981), *Corporate Crime*, New York.
Leonard, E. B. (1982), *Women, Crime and Society*, New York.
Sutherland, E. H. (1983), *White Collar Crime: The Uncut Version*, New Haven.
Taylor, I., Walton, P. and Young, J. (1973), *The New Criminology*, London.
See also: *criminology; deviance; labelling theory; punishment.*

Criminology

There are two scriptural beginnings to the history of criminology, each marking out a somewhat different fate for the study of crime and its control. The first dates from the mid-eighteenth century and tells of the revolutionary contribution of Enlightenment thinkers like Beccaria and Bentham in breaking with a previously 'archaic', 'barbaric', 'repressive' or 'arbitrary' system of criminal law. This was the classical school.

For these reformers, legal philosophers and political theorists, the crime question was dominantly the punishment question. Their programme was to prevent punishment from being, in Beccaria's words, 'an act of violence of one or many against a private citizen'; instead it should be 'essentially public, prompt, necessary, the least possible in given circumstances, proportionate to the crime, dictated by laws'. Classicism presented a model of rationality: on the one side, the free 'sovereign' individual acting according to the dictates of reason and self interest; on the other, the limited liberal state, contracted to grant rights and liberties, to prescribe duties and to impose the fair and just punishment that must result from the knowing infliction of social harm.

This 'immaculate conception' account of the birth of classicism has been challenged by revisionist histories of law and the state. Dates, concepts and subjects have been reordered. Classicism is now to be understood in terms of the broader rationalization of crime control associated with the emergence of the free market and the new capitalist order. But the preoccupations of classicism − whether they appear in utilitarianism, Kantianism, liberalism, anarchism or indeed any political philosophy at all − have remained a constant thread in criminology. This is where the subject overlaps with politics, jurisprudence and the history and sociology of the law.

A century after classicism, though, criminology was to claim for itself another beginning and another set of influences. This was the positivist revolution − dated in comic-book intellectual history with the publication in 1876 of Lombroso's *Delinquent Man*. This was a 'positivism' which shared the more general social-scientific connotations of the term (the notion, that is, of the unity of the scientific method) but which acquired in criminology a more specific meaning. As David Matza suggests in his standard sociologies of criminological knowledge (Matza, 1964 and 1969), criminological positivism managed the astonishing feat of separating the study of crime from the contemplation of the state. Classicism was dismissed as mere metaphysical speculation. The new programme was to focus not on the crime (the act) but the criminal (the actor); it was to assume not rationality, free will and choice, but determinism (biological, psychic or social). At the centre of the criminological enterprise now was the notion of causality. No longer a sovereign being, subject to more or less the same pulls and pushes as his fellow citizens, the criminal was now a special person or member of a special class.

The whole of the last century of criminology can be understood as a series of creative, even brilliant, yet eventually repetitive variations on these late nineteenth-century themes. The particular image conjured up by Lombroso's criminal type – the atavistic genetic throwback – faded away, but the subsequent structure and logic of criminological explanation remained largely within the positivist paradigm. Whether the level of explanation was biological, psychological, sociological or a combination of these ('multifactorial' as some versions were dignified), the Holy Grail was a general causal theory: why do people commit crime? This quest gave the subject its collective self definition: 'the scientific study of the causes of crime'.

At each stage of this search, criminology strengthened its claim to exist as an autonomous, multidisciplinary subject. Somewhat like a parasite, criminology attached itself to its host subjects (notably, law, psychology, psychiatry and sociology) and drew from them methods, theories and academic credibility. At the same time – somewhat like a colonial power landing on new territory – each of these disciplines descended on the eternally fascinating subjects of crime and punishment and claimed them as its own. In this fashion, criminological theories and methods draw on Freudianism, behaviourism, the Chicago school of sociology, functionalism, anomie theory, interactionism, Marxism and much else. Each of these traces can be found in any current criminology textbook; it would be difficult to think of a major system of thought in the social sciences which would not be so represented.

All the time this positivist trajectory was being established, criminologists retained their interest in the question of punishment. If, in a sense, all criminology became positivist, then also all criminology remained concerned with 'classical' matters. But instead of speculation about the limits and nature of the criminal sanction, this side of criminology (sometimes called penology) took this sanction as politically given. True, there was (and still is) an important debate about whether the subject matter of criminology should be confined to conventional legal definitions of crime or shifted to include all forms of socially injurious conduct. The punishment question, however, was largely resolved in empirical terms: describing, analysing and evaluating the workings of the criminal justice system. Research findings were built up about the police, courts, prisons and various other agencies devoted to the prevention, control, deterrence or treatment of crime. This remains today the major part of the criminological enterprise.

Little of this, however, was 'pure' empiricism. The classical tradition was alive in another sense: modern criminologists became the heirs of the Enlightenment beliefs in rationality and progress. Their scientific task was carried along by a sense of faith: that the business of crime and delinquency control could be made not only more efficient, but also more humane. As reformers, advisers and consultants, criminologists claim for themselves not merely an autonomous body of knowledge, but the status of an applied science or even a profession.

It is this simultaneous claim to knowledge and power which links the two sides of criminology: causation and control. In positivism, this is an organic link: to know the cause is to know the right policy. Recently, however, both this link and its justification in the immaculate-conception history of positivism have been questioned. Histories of the emergence of the prison in the late eighteenth and early nineteenth century have shown the dependence of control systems on theories of rehabilitation, behaviour modification and anomie well before their supposed 'discovery' by scientific criminology. To critics like Foucault (1977) criminological knowledge has always been wholly utilitarian: an elaborate alibi to justify the exercise of power.

In the general climate of radical self-scrutiny which descended on the social sciences in the 1960s, criminology, too, began to fragment a little. There were three major attacks against the positivist hegemony – each in its peculiar and quite distinct way representing a return to classical questions.

(1) Labelling theory – a loose body of ideas derived from symbolic interactionism – restated some simple sociological truths about the relative nature of social rules and the normative boundaries which they mark. Crime was one form of that wider

category of social action, deviance; criminology should be absorbed into the sociology of deviance. Beyond such conceptual and disciplinary boundary disputes, the very nature of the conventional quest for causality was regarded with scepticism. In addition to the standard behavioural question (why do some people do these bad things?) there were a series of definitional questions: Why are certain actions defined as rule breaking? How are these rules applied? And what are the consequences of this application? At times, these definitional questions seemed to attain causal primacy: it was not that control led to deviance, but deviance to control. Social control agencies – with their organized systems of labelling, stigmatizing and isolation – were meddlesome busybodies, making matters worse for society and its underdogs and outsiders. And behind the pretentions of scientific criminology was a simple-minded identification with middle-class values.

(2) This liberal criticism of liberalism was to become harder and tighter in the second onslaught on mainstream criminology. This came from what has been labelled variously as 'conflict', 'new', 'critical', 'radical', or 'Marxist' criminology. Drawing initially on some strands of labelling theory and conflict sociology and on the classical Marxist writing about law, class and the state, these theories moved even further from the agenda of positivism. Traditional causal questions were either dismissed or made subservient to the assumed criminogenic features of capitalism. Legalistic definitions were either expanded to include crimes of the powerful (those social harms which the state licences itself to commit), or else subjected to historicist and materialist enquiry. Labelling theory's wider notion of deviance was abandoned. Law was the only important mode of control, and the focus of criminology had to be shifted to the power of the state to criminalize certain actions rather than others. The analytical task was to construct a political economy of crime and its control. The normative task (that is, the solution to the crime problem) was to eliminate those economic and political systems of exploitation which gave rise to crime. The goal was a crime-free society, possible only under a

different social order and impossible with the conceptual tools of bourgeois criminology.

(3) Another critique of the positivist enterprise came from a quite different theoretical and political direction. Impressed by the apparent failure of the causal quest and of progressive policies such as treatment, rehabilitation and social reform, a loose coalition of intellectuals appeared under such rallying calls as 'realism', 'back to justice' and 'neo-classicism'. Some of them are neo-liberals – and theirs is a note of sad disenchantment with the ideas and policies of progressive criminology. Some of them are conservatives (or neo-conservatives) – and theirs is a note of satisfaction about the supposed failures of liberalism. Both these wings harken back to classical questions; the notion of justice (or 'just deserts') allows liberals to talk of rights, equity and fairness, while it allows conservatives to talk about law and order, social defence, deterrence and the protection of society. In neither case – but particularly for conservatives – is there much interest in traditional questions of causation.

Criminology is a subject with a complicated past and a polemical present. Most criminologists are employed at the core of the enterprise: busy either describing, classifying and explaining crime or else analysing, evaluating and advocating policy. At the periphery, are various fascinating intellectual disputes about the subject's true content and justification. As Jock Young has recently shown (1981), the major schools of criminological thought are divided on quite basic issues: the image of human nature, the basis of social order, the nature and extent of crime, the relationship between theory and policy. And if we move out of the Anglo-American cultures in which contemporary criminology has mainly flourished, even more fundamental differences appear (a major – and belated – recent development has been the serious comparative analysis of crime and its control).

But whether positivist or neoclassical, radical or conservative, detached intellectuals or disguised policemen, criminologists confront the same questions. All this diversity is a manifestation of a single tension: crime is behaviour, but it is behaviour which the state is organized to punish.

Stanley Cohen
Hebrew University of Jerusalem

References
Foucault, M. (1977 [1975]), *Discipline and Punish*, London.
(Original French edn, *Surveiller et punir*, Paris.)
Matza, D. (1964), *Delinquency and Drift*, New York.
Matza, D. (1969), *Becoming Deviant*, Englewood Cliffs, N.J.
Young, J. (1981), 'Thinking seriously about crime' in M.
Fitzgerald *et al.* (eds), *Crime and Society*, London.

Further Reading
Christie, N. (1981), *Limits to Pain*, Oxford.
Sutherland, E. and Cressey, D. (1984), *Principles of Criminology*,
Philadelphia.
Sykes, G. (1978), *Criminology*, New York.
See also: *crime and delinquency; labelling theory; penology;
punishment.*

Deviance

Although the word *deviance* has been employed for over three hundred years, its sociological meanings are rather recent and distinct. In the main, sociologists and criminologists have taken deviance to refer to behaviour that is banned, censured, stigmatized or penalized. It is often portrayed as a breaking of rules. It is considered more extensive than crime, crime being no more than a breach of one particular kind of rule, but it includes crime and its outer margins are unclear and imprecise. What exactly deviance comprises, what it excludes, what makes it interesting, and how it should be characterized, are not settled. There have been studies of very diverse groups in the name of the sociology of deviance. There have been descriptions of the deaf, the blind, the ill, the mad, dwarves, stutterers, strippers, prostitutes, homosexuals, thieves, murderers, nudists and drug addicts. Sociologists are not in accord about whether all these roles are unified and what it is that may be said to unify them. They can appeal to no common convention within their own discipline. Neither can they turn to lay definitions for guidance. On the contrary, commonplace interpretations are often elastic, contingent and local. What is called deviant can shift from time to time and place to place, its significance being unstable.

Common sense and everyday talk do not seem to point to an area that is widely and unambiguously recognized as deviant. It is not even evident that people *do* talk about deviance with any great frequency. Instead, they allude to specific forms of conduct without appearing to claim that there is a single, over-arching category that embraces them all. They may talk of punks, addicts, glue-sniffers, extremists, thieves, traitors, liars and eccentrics, but they rarely mention *deviants*. It may only be the sociologist who finds it interesting and instructive to clump these groups together under a solitary title.

The apparent elusiveness and vagueness of the idea of deviance has elicited different responses from sociologists. Some have refrained from attempting to find one definition that covers every instance of the phenomenon. They have used *ad hoc* or implied definitions that serve the analytic needs of the moment and suppress the importance of definition itself. Others, like Liazos, have questioned the intellectual integrity of the subject, alleging that it may amount to little more than an incoherent jumble of 'nuts, sluts and perverts'. Phillipson has actually described the analysis of deviance as 'that antediluvian activity which sought to show oddities, curiosities, peccadilloes and villains as central to sociological reason'.

A number of sociologists have chosen to represent 'that ante-diluvian activity' as important precisely because its subject is so odd: the inchoate character of deviance becomes a remarkable property of the phenomenon rather than a weakness in its description. Matza, for example, held that 'plural evaluation, shifting standards, and moral ambiguity may, and do, coexist with a phenomenal realm that is commonly sensed as deviant'. His book, *Becoming Deviant* (1969), proceeded to chart the special contours of that realm by following the passage of an archetypal deviant into its interior. In such a guise, deviance is taken to offer a rare glimpse of the fluid and contradictory face of society, showing things in unexpected relief and proportion. Garfinkel, Goffman and others have taken to repairing to the deviant margins because they offer new perspectives through incongruity or strain, perspectives that jolt the understanding and make the sociologist 'stumble into awareness'. Deviants are required to negotiate problems of meaning and structure that are a little foreign to everyday life. The study of their activity may force the sociologist to view the world as anthropologically strange. Indeed, some sociologists have implicitly turned the social world inside out, making deviance the centre and the centre peripheral. They have explored the odd and the exotic, giving birth to a sociology of the absurd that dwells on the parts played by indeterminacy, paradox and surprise in social life.

Absurdity is perhaps given its fullest recognition in a number of essays by structuralists and phenomenologists. It is there asserted that deviance is distinguished by its special power to muddle and unsettle social reality. Deviation is described by its ability to upset systems of thought and methods of classification. Deviant matters are things out of place, things that make no sense. As Scott argued, 'The property of deviance is conferred on things that are perceived as being anomalous . . .' The meaninglessness of deviance is thus forced to become substantially more than a simple lack of intellectual coherence in sociology. People are thought to find it disturbing, and phenomenologists have replied by turning their gaze towards the problems which disturbance can raise. The phenomenologists' difference with Marxist and radical sociologists probably turns on their emphasis on flux and disorder. Radical sociologists tend to stress the solidity of the social world and the importance of what Gouldner called 'overpowering social structures'. Phenomenologists and others tend to stress the openness and plasticity of things, arguing that social structure is actually rather delicate and negotiable.

What *is* certain is that the analysis of deviance echoes many of the unities and disunities of sociology at large. Sociological definition is not neutral and independent. It will refract wider debates, problems and pursuits. It is in this sense that sociologists do not necessarily mean the same thing when they talk of deviance. Their ideas sometimes contradict one another, although contradiction is often no more than a trick of language, an effect of the different vocabularies that have become attached to theories.

A list of examples should reveal a little of that diversity.

Probably the most elementary definition of deviance describes it as behaviour that is *statistically infrequent*. A contrast is traced between the normal, which is common, and the abnormal or deviant, which is uncommon. That definition is deployed characteristically in clinical or psychological analysis that relies on counting: normal distribution curves are drawn, and the deviant is that which falls at the poles. Those who wet their beds with unusual frequency, who are very tall or very short, who read obsessively or not at all are deviant for practical numerical purposes. It is a definition that serves well enough in certain settings, but it can sometimes fail to make sense of deviance as it is presented in everyday life. Thus, the statistically infrequent may be socially unremarked and inconsequential. The statistically frequent may be exposed to control, disapproval and stigma. What is *assumed* to be infrequent, acquiring some of its identity from that assumption, may actually be quite common. (Homosexuality, adultery and chastity are all rather more abundant than many people suppose, but they are *taken* to be unusual.) It may indeed be *beliefs* about statistical incidence that are occasionally more significant than the incidence itself. Statistical analysis can then be rephrased to produce a commentary about the interplay between ideas about deviance and convention.

A second major strand of sociological thought is *Marxism*, but many Marxists have relegated deviance to the margins of analysis. Its pettiness has been emphasized both in the explicit arguments of some sociologists and in the practical neglect of deviance by others. Deviation is commonly thought to be a process that is relatively trivial in a world that is dominated by the massive structures of political economy. It has been maintained that little can be gained from studying deviance that cannot be achieved more directly, efficiently and elegantly from the analysis of class and state. Some, like Hirst, Bankowski and Mungham, have actually reproached Marxist and radical sociologists of deviance for discussing inappropriate and minor problems. Marxists, they claim, should concentrate on the class struggle.

When Marxists *do* explore deviance, they tend to stress its bearing on the class struggle and the state. Thus Hill, Thompson and Hobsbawm have developed a social history of crime that emphasizes the scale of popular opposition to the emergence of capitalism in England. Hall, Cohen and Willis have talked of youthful deviance as 'resistance through ritual', a fleeting and probably doomed act of refusal to accede to the authority of institutions that oppress the working class. Sumner has taken the unity of deviance to stem from the censures that reside in the core of capitalist ideology; Taylor has lodged the origins of deviance in the contradictions of the ailing political economy of late capitalism in crisis; Platt and Quinney cast deviants as those who have been defeated in the class war; Box and Pearce present them as the scapegoats who divert the gaze from the major pathologies of capitalism; and so it goes on. Marxists deposit deviation in a world made up of resistance, protest and conflict. Few have occupied themselves with processes outside that world. After all, that is the world of Marxism. Lea and Young *have* ventured outside but their place within Marxism may have become a little unsure in consequence.

A third major representative strand is *functionalism*, and Talcott Parsons is the pivot of functionalism. Parsons typified one version of deviance as the disorganized phenomena that can attend institutions and individuals that have become out of joint. He argued that, as the social world changes, so its parts may move with unequal velocities and in different directions, straining against one another and creating problems of cohesion. Deviance then became activity that sprang from defective integration. It could evolve to become a new conformity; persist as a source of stress within the social system; or disappear altogether as coherence returned to society.

Parsons also focused on a very special form of deviance in his essay on the 'sick role'. He depicted illness as the status of those who should not be rewarded for occupying what could become a dangerously seductive and useless position. The sick are pampered and, without discouragement, people might learn to malinger. Illness had to be controlled by the threat of stigma.

Almost all other functionalists have diverged from Parsons's insistence on the dysfunctions of deviance. Instead, they have elected to illustrate the surprising fashion in which deviation has unintentionally buttressed the social order. Durkheim pointed to the solidarity conferred by collective sentiments outraged by the breaking of rules. Erikson wrote of how dramatized encounters between deviants and agents of social control beat the bounds of the moral community. Deviance was to be described as a dialectical foil to themes that infuse the moral centre of society. Without a vividly reproduced deviance, it was held, the centre would lose its structure and integrity. Good requires the bad, God Satan, and morality immorality. Within the borders of society, too, deviance was to be depicted as a kind of dangerous but necessary zone between major regions and classes of phenomena. The revulsion said to surround the homosexual and the hermaphrodite enforces morally charged divisions between the genders. Deviance then supports convention, and it does so in numerous ways. Bell and Merton talked of the part played by organized crime in repairing economic and political defects in America, suggesting that the criminal offers power, influence and services where none is provided by the respectable order. Davis remarked how prostitution supports monogamy and bastardy primogeniture. Most functionalist essays on deviance are brief and unsystematic. Yet their recurrent theme is that deviance upholds what it seems to disrupt. Their paradox is the interesting symbiosis of rule-making, rule-enforcement and rule-breaking.

There are other postures: feminists writing about the rooting of deviation in patriarchy; control theorists taking deviance to be the wildness that erupts when social disciplines become weak; and ecologists charting the interlacing of deviance and conformity in the lives of people who live in the same territory.

Each gives rule-breaking a place in a distinct theoretical environment. Each imparts a distinctiveness that is sometimes quite marked and sometimes a little superficial. Without much effort, it is quite possible to transcribe some of those definitions so that they begin to resemble one another more closely. Thus functionalism resonates the assertions made by Marxists about the interdependence of crime and capitalism, by feminists about the links between patriarchy and rule-breaking, and by phenomenologists about the work done in the social regulation of anomaly.

The sociology of deviance has probably been allied most prominently to the symbolic interactionism, labelling theory and phenomenology that came to the fore in the 1960s. So intimate is that connexion that the sociology of deviance is often taken to be a wholly interactionist undertaking, bearing with it a crowd of unstated assumptions about methods, history and focus. *Deviance* is then held to refer not only to rule-breaking but also to a special method of interpreting rule-breaking. Those who chose to explore deviance in the late 1950s, 1960s and 1970s sought to advertise their distance from criminologists described as 'positivist' and 'correctionalist'. They took their task to be the symbolic reconstruction of deviance, learning how rule-breaking had become possible, what meanings it attained, and how it progressed from stage to stage. The cast of performers was enlarged to include all those who significantly affected critical passages in the evolution of deviant histories. The influence of people and events was held to change with each new phase, being interpreted and reinterpreted by participants. Developments were thought to be intelligible only within the emergent logic of an unfolding career. The importance of interpretation, the processual character of social life and the centrality of deviant identity led interactionists to redefine deviation as a moving transaction between those who made rules, those who broke rules and those who implemented rules. Deviance was held to be *negotiated* over time, its properties reflecting the practical power and assumptions of those who propelled it from phase to phase. At the very core of the negotiating process are deviants themselves, and their conduct responds to the attitudes which are taken towards them at various junctures. Becoming deviant entails a recasting of the self and a redrafting of motives. It entails a supplying of accounts, meanings, purposes and character. In that process, deviant and conventional identities are manufactured, and the interactionist sociologists of deviance furnished portrait after portrait of hustlers, police officers, prostitutes, delinquents and drug users. Their work continues although it has become a little overshadowed by more recent models of conduct.

Paul Rock
London School of Economics and Political Science

References

Bankowski, Z., Mungham, G. and Young, P. (1977), 'Radical criminology or radical criminologist?', *Contemporary Crises*, 1.

Becker, H. (1963), *Outsiders*, New York.

Bell, D. (1960), *The End of Ideology*, New York.

Cohen, P. (1972), 'Working class youth cultures in East London', in *Working Papers in Cultural Studies*, Birmingham.

Davis, K. (1961), 'Prostitution' in R. Merton and R. Nisbet (eds), *Contemporary Social Problems*, New York.

Downes, D. and Rock, P. (1982), *Understanding Deviance*, Oxford.

Durkheim, E. (1933), *The Division of Labour in Society*, New York *(De la Division du travail social*, 1893, Paris).

Erikson, K. (1966), *Wayward Puritans*, New York.

Garfinkel, H. (1967), *Studies in Ethnomethodology*, Englewood Cliffs, N.J.

Goffman, E. (1963), *Stigma*, Englewood Cliffs, N.J.

Gouldner, A. (1970), *The Coming Crisis in Western Sociology*, New York.

Hall, S. *et al.* (eds) (1976), *Resistance Through Ritual*, London.

Hill, C. (1961), *The Century of Revolution*, Edinburgh.

Hirst, P. (1975), 'Marx and Engels on law, crime and morality', in I. Taylor *et al.* (eds), *Critical Criminology*, London.

Hobsbawm, E. (1965), *Primitive Rebels*, New York.

Lea, J. and Young, J. (1984), *What Is To Be Done About Law and Order?*, London.

Merton, R. (1957), *Social Theory and Social Structure*, New York.

Parsons, T. (1951), *The Social System*, New York.

Platt, A. (1978), '"Street Crime" – A view from the Left', *Crime and Social Justice*, 9.

Quinney, R. (1975), 'Crime control in capitalist society', in I. Taylor *et al.* (eds), *Critical Criminology*, London.

Scott, R. (1972), 'A proposed framework for analyzing deviance as a property of social order', in R. Scott and J. Douglas (eds), *Theoretical Perspectives on Deviance*, New York.

Scott, R. and Douglas, J. (eds) (1972), *Theoretical Perspectives on Deviance*, New York.

Smart, C. (1977), *Women, Crime and Criminology*, London.

Sumner, C. (1976), 'Ideology and deviance', Ph.D. Dissertation, Sheffield.

Taylor, I. (1980), 'The law and order issue in the British General Election and the Canadian Federal Election of 1979', *Canadian Journal of Sociology*.

Taylor, I., Walton, P. and Young, J. (1973), *The New Criminology*, London.

Thompson, E. (1975), *Whigs and Hunters*, London.

Willis, P. (1977), *Learning to Labour*, Farnborough.

Divorce

Divorce is an institutionalized way of voluntarily ending a marriage. There are other forms of voluntary marital dissolution, such as desertion or a mutually-agreed-upon separation; but divorce differs in that it is officially sanctioned by the state or the ruling group, and it allows both partners to remarry. The institution of divorce was present in many preindustrial societies and exists in most countries today. As Goode (1956) noted, '*All* family systems have *some* kinds of escape mechanisms built into them, to permit individuals to survive the pressures of the system, and one of these is divorce.'

Nevertheless, the levels of divorce and the reasons for divorce have varied widely from society to society. In some traditional Islamic societies, divorce was easy to obtain (at least for males) and quite common; in other traditional societies, such as China before the twentieth century, divorce was rather rare. Social and economic development has often brought a lowering of divorce levels in societies where it was quite common, and an increase in societies where it was quite uncommon (Goode, 1963).

In the West, the divorce rate has risen from a relatively low level in the preindustrial era to the current high level. This process accelerated in the 1960s and 1970s, leading to widespread concern about the future of marriage, but, since the mid-1970s, the rate of increase in divorce appears to have slowed down. In the US, which has the highest divorce rate of the developed nations, about one out of two marriages will end in divorce if current rates continue.

The reasons for Western divorce are different now from the past. Previously, a divorce was granted when one partner failed to fulfil an important responsibility: sexual fidelity, economic support, and so forth. But in many Western countries, divorces are now granted on the basis of incompatibility, without the need for either partner to be legally at fault. This shift toward 'no-fault' divorce reflects a changing view of marriage from an 'institution to a companionship' in the famous phrase of Burgess and Locke (1945). Marriage is defined less as a contractual arrangement in which each partner must carry out certain tasks, and more as a partnership in which both partners primarily seek emotional gratification. When that gratification is lacking, either partner may feel justified in seeking a divorce. The Western view of marriage and divorce has changed because of rising standards of living, the greater economic independence of women from men, the higher expectations couples have about marriage, and the decrease in the stigma of being divorced.

Because of the rise in divorce in the West, three family forms are becoming dominant: families of first marriages, single-parent families (usually a mother and children), and families formed by remarriages after divorce. Divorce remains a traumatic event, at least in the short run, for those who experience it. Much current research is directed at the effects of parental divorce on children. It is clear that the short-run effects are quite traumatic (Wallerstein and Kelly, 1980); but the long-term effects are not yet clear.

Andrew Cherlin
Johns Hopkins University

References
Burgess, E. W. and Locke, H. J. (1945), *The Family: From Institution to Companionship*, New York.
Goode, W. J. (1956), *Women in Divorce*, New York.
Goode, W. J. (1963), *World Revolution and Family Patterns*, New York.
Wallerstein, J. S. and Kelly, J. B. (1980), *Surviving the Breakup: How Children and Parents Cope with Divorce*, New York.

Further Reading
Cherlin, A. J. (1981), *Marriage, Divorce, Remarriage*, Cambridge, Mass.
Chester, R. (ed.) (1977), *Divorce in Europe*, The Hague.
Levinger, G. and Moles, O. C. (eds) (1979), *Divorce and Separation: Context, Causes, and Consequences*, New York.

Drug Use
The ingestion of mind-altering substances is very nearly a human universal; in practically every society, a sizeable proportion of its members take at least one drug for psychoactive purposes (Weil, 1972). This has been true for a significant stretch of history. Fermentation was one of the earliest of discoveries, predating the fashioning of metal; humans have been ingesting alcoholic beverages for some 10,000 years. Several dozen plants contain chemicals that influence the workings of the mind, and have been smoked, chewed or sniffed by members of societies all over the world. These plants include coca leaves, the opium poppy, marijuana, the psilocybin mushroom, the peyote cactus, quat leaves, nutmeg, tobacco, coffee beans, tea leaves, and the cocoa bean. During the past century or more, hundreds of thousands of psychoactive chemicals have been discovered, isolated or synthesized by scientists or phys-

icians. Thousands have been marketed for medicinal purposes. According to the journal, *Pharmacy Times*, approximately 1.5 billion medical prescriptions for drugs are written each year in the United States alone. Although most of these drugs are not psychoactive, roughly one out of six of these prescriptions is written for a substance that significantly alters the workings of the human mind. Drug-taking is one of the more widespread of human activities.

Most of the time that psychoactive chemicals are ingested, they are used 'in a culturally approved manner' (Edgerton, 1976), with little or no negative impact on the user or on society. However, in a significant minority of cases, drugs are taken in a culturally unacceptable or disapproved fashion: a condemned drug is taken instead of an approved one, it is taken too frequently or under the wrong circumstances, for the wrong reasons, or with undesirable consequences. With the establishment of the modern nation-state and, along with it, the elaboration of an explicit legal code, certain actions came to be deemed illegal or criminal. The use, possession or sale of certain kinds of drugs, taking drugs in certain contexts, or the ingestion of drugs for disapproved motives, have been regarded as crimes in nearly all countries, punished with a fine or imprisonment of the offender. The catch-all term 'abuse' is commonly used to refer to somewhat different types of drug use: (1) any use of an illegal drug for non-medical purposes, or (2) any use of a drug, legal or illegal, to the point where it becomes a threat to the user's physical or mental well-being, or interferes with major life goals or functioning, such as educational or occupational achievement, or marriage. 'Misuse' is the term that is commonly used to refer to the inappropriate use of a legal prescription drug for medical purposes.

It must be emphasized that drug use is not a unitary phenomenon. There are, to begin with, different types of drugs, classified according to their action. Drugs are commonly categorized on the basis of their impact on the central nervous system (the CNS) – the brain and spinal cord. Some drugs speed up signals passing through the CNS; they are called *stimulants* and include cocaine, the amphetamines, caffeine, and nicotine. Other drugs retard signals passing through the CNS, and are called *depress-ants*. Depressants include *narcotics* (such as opium, heroin, and morphine), which dull the sensation of pain, *sedatives* (such as alcohol, the barbiturates, and mathaqualone) and 'minor' *tranquillizers* (such as Valium), which reduce anxiety, and 'major' tranquillizers or *antipsychotics*, which inhibit the manifestation of symptoms of psychosis, especially schizophrenia. Hallucinogens (such as LSD) and marijuana do not fit neatly into this stimulant-depressant continuum.

Psychoactive drugs, even of the same type, are taken for a variety of reasons: to attain religious or mystical ecstasy, to suppress fatigue, hunger, or anxiety, to enhance hedonism and pleasure, to heal the body or the mind, to facilitate socializing or interpersonal intimacy, to follow the dictates of a particular group or subculture; and to establish an identity as a certain kind of person. A drug's psychoactive properties may be central to the user's motive for taking it, or incidental to it; the intoxication may be experienced for intrinsic reasons (that is, the drug is taken by the user to get 'high') or the drug taken for instrumental purposes (that is, to attain a specific goal, such as alleviating pain). Of the many varieties of drug use, perhaps the three most common and important are: (1) legal recreational use, (2) illegal recreational use, and (3) legal medical use. Each of these modes of use will attract strikingly different users and will have strikingly different consequences. Even the same drug will be used by a different set of individuals for entirely different purposes with different effects. It is a fallacy to assume that the pharmacological properties of a drug dictate the consequences following its use; factors such as the motives for its use, the social context in which use is embedded, social norms surrounding use, methods of use, and so on, all play a major role in a drug's impact on the individual and on society. It is misleading, therefore, to assume that the use of even the same drug in different cultural settings will result in the same effects, consequences or impact. In parts of India, for example, holy men (*sadhus*) smoke cannabis to quell their appetite for food and sex; in the West, the same drug is successfully used to enhance precisely the same appetites.

(1) *Legal recreational use* refers to the attempt to alter one's consciousness by ingesting a psychoactive substance whose possession is not against the law. For the most part, in Western nations, this refers mainly to alcohol consumption. When the term 'drug' is used to apply to substances consumed outside a medical context, it usually connotes those whose use is illegal and/or strongly condemned and disvalued. It rarely refers to substances such as alcohol. Although not generally perceived or regarded as a drug, alcohol qualifies for the term in a pharmacological and a physiological sense: not only is it psychoactive, and widely used for this reason, but it can produce a physical dependence, or 'addiction', in heavy, long-term, chronic users, and it causes or is associated with a wide range of medical maladies. Many estimates place the proportion of alcoholics at roughly one drinker in ten, and argue that alcoholism is the West's most serious drug problem. In short, alcohol is 'a drug by any other name' (Fort, 1973).

(2) Of all types of drug use, *illegal recreational use* attracts the most public attention and interest. In the two decades following the early 1960s, Western Europe and North America experienced an unprecedented rise in the recreational use of illegal psychoactive drugs. The most widely used of these drugs are marijuana and hashish, products of the plant *Cannabis sativa*. In most countries, there are as many episodes of cannabis use as episodes of the use of all other illegal drugs combined. And of all illegal drugs, cannabis is the one that users are most likely to continue using regularly, and least likely to abandon or use extremely episodically. Of all illegal drugs, marijuana is the one with the highest ratio of current to lifetime users. In one study, 52 per cent of all at least one-time marijuana users had taken this drug one or more times in the past month; for cocaine, this was 34 per cent, for the other stimulants, 19 per cent, for the hallucinogens, 18 per cent, and for the sedatives, 16 per cent (Fishburne *et al.*, 1980). Cannabis is the illegal drug that people most frequently 'stick with'. As with alcohol, the majority of users take the drug in a fairly moderate, controlled fashion. Approximately 10 per cent of all cannabis users become so involved with their drug of choice that it becomes an

obsession or a psychological dependency, threatening their health and occupational or educational attainment. While the recreational use of more dangerous drugs, such as heroin, cocaine, and barbiturates, is considerably less than for cannabis, the potential for abuse of these substances is far greater. It is estimated that there are as many as half a million heroin addicts in the United States alone (Goode, 1984).

(3) The *medical use* of psychoactive chemicals in the Western world has undergone dramatic changes over the past century. Late in the nineteenth century, over-the-counter preparations containing psychoactive substances such as morphine and cocaine were freely available and were widely used to treat or cure medical ailments. Legal controls on what these nostrums contained were practically non-existent. When authorities became aware of widespread abuses of these drugs, dispensing them became tightly controlled, and medical prescriptions became necessary to obtain them. In the United States, the number of prescriptions written for psychoactive drugs rose steadily until the early 1970s when, again, misuse and abuse of these substances was publicized. Since that time, there has been a steep decline in the number of psychoactive drug doses dispensed by physicians. For instance, in the United States in 1975, 61.3 million prescriptions were written for Valium, that nation's number one prescription drug; in 1980, this figure had dropped to 33.6 million (Rosenblatt, 1982). The number of prescriptions written for morphine in 1981 was half the number for 1976. Benzedrine, a once popular stimulant, was prescribed one-sixth as often in 1981 as in 1976 (Goode, 1984). There has been a dramatic downward trend in the use of psychoactive prescription drugs between the 1970s and the 1980s; the trend continues unabated. With some of these drugs, such as the barbiturates, this cut-back has translated into a decline in illegal recreational or 'street' usage; with other drugs, such as methaqualone and amphetamine, this has not taken place.

In contrast, the treatment of psychotic disorders, mainly schizophrenia, with the use of anti-psychotic drugs such as Thorazine, has been increasing dramatically since their discovery in the 1950s. The impact of the medical use of anti-psychotic drugs, also called 'major' tranquillizers, can be measured by the dramatic decline in the number of resident patients in mental hospitals. Between 1945 and 1955, in the United States, there was a yearly average increase of 13,000 patients residing in state mental hospitals; in the latter year, the total was just under 560,000. Between 1954 and 1955, psychoactive agents were introduced as treatment for psychosis. Because of the success of this modality in controlling the symptoms of schizophrenia, patients who were previously confined in hospitals were released as outpatients. By 1978, the number of resident state mental hospital patients in the United States had plumetted to under 150,000 (Ray, 1983). The average length of hospitalization dropped from six months in 1955 to 26 days in 1976. The decline in the number of mental patients in hospitals can be traced directly to the use of anti-psychotic or phenothiazine drugs, the 'major' tranquillizers.

Erich Goode
State University of New York at Stony Brook

References

Edgerton, R. B. (1976), *Deviance: A Cross-Cultural Perspective*, Menlo Park, Calif.

Fishburne, P. M. *et al.* (1980), *National Survey on Drug Abuse: Main Findings, 1979*, Rockville, Maryland.

Fort, J. (1973), *Alcohol: Our Biggest Drug Problem*, New York.

Goode, E. (1984), *Drugs in American Society*, 2nd edn, New York.

Ray, O. (1983), *Drugs, Society, and Human Behavior*, 3rd edn, St Louis.

Rosenblatt, J. (1982), 'Prescription-drug abuse', *Editorial Research Reports*, 1.

Weil, A. (1972), *The Natural Mind: A New Way of Looking at Drugs and the Higher Consciousness*, Boston.

Further Reading

Abel, E. L. (1982), *Marihuana: The First Twelve Thousand Years*, New York.

Grinspoon, L. and Bakalar, J. B. (1979), *Psychedelic Drugs Reconsidered*, New York.

Judson, H. F. (1974), *Heroin Addiction in Britain*, New York.

Young, J. (1971), *The Drugtakers: The Social Meaning of Drug Use*, London.

See also: *alcoholism*.

Ethnic Groups

Segments of a population form ethnic groups by virtue of sharing the combination of (a) common descent (real or supposed), (b) a socially relevant cultural or physical characteristic, and (c) a set of attitudes and behaviours.

On this definition, people are usually born to an ethnic group rather than acquiring their ethnic status through a special act. Most marry within and remain part of the ethnic group of origin throughout their entire lives even if mobility is feasible (as in the case of religious conversion). Since ethnic group members are actually or putatively related to one another by blood ties, an ethnic group is a kind of a super-extended family.

A primary basis for differentiation between ethnic groups can be either cultural – such as a language, a nationality and a religion – or physical – such as skin pigmentation and body shape – or both. The distinguishing feature is considered significant in the society, and people use it in differentiating themselves from others.

Members of an ethnic group also share certain feelings, ideas and behaviours. To form a real ethnic group and not just a mere ethnic collection of people, people must, at least to some degree, perceive themselves as a distinct ethnic group ('we' and 'they' feelings), sense a common fate, interact more among themselves than with outsiders, and think and behave similarly.

Ethnicity is not presumed to exist when any of these defining criteria is missing. Lacking an idea of common descent, women, the disabled, the sane, or nonbelievers, should not be regarded as ethnic groups although each of these categories of people is distinguished by evident cultural or biological traits, and even by certain attitudes and behaviours.

Furthermore, a distinct characteristic becomes ethnically

relevant only when people apply it to mark themselves off from others or when it is used to impose an identity by outsiders. In India, for instance, speakers of different languages intermingled freely for centuries. Linguistically based ethnic groups emerged there only after the British established administrative divisions, which in 1948 turned into provincial states, along linguistic lines, so creating linguistic majorities and minorities. To cite another example, in Nazi Germany Jews were forced into a status of a racial group.

Ethnic groups should also be distinguished from social classes. A social class is a group of people who share the same level of resources, such as education, income, prestige and power, or work in the same occupational category (such as blue-collar jobs). According to another view, a social class is constituted by persons who hold similar positions in the process of production (workers, employers). Since social classes are groups of unequal statuses and ethnic groups are descent groups, they can cross-cut each other. A social class may include members of different ethnic groups, and an ethnic group may include members of different social classes. Commonly, however, ethnic groups and social classes overlap appreciably.

Formation

Ethnicity crystallizes only in situations where people of different backgrounds come into contact or share the same institutions or political system. Villagers or tribesmen in isolated areas, or citizens in homogeneous states like Portugal, are not members of ethnic groups.

Ethnic divisions are evident throughout human history, yet they became more pervasive in recent times because technological advances multiplied intergroup contacts and brought together hitherto separate peoples. The great historical forces that fashioned the world ethnic mosaic are colonialism, imperialism, annexation, involuntary migration, free emigration and nationalism. European expansion into overseas colonies formed a division between the white settlers and the indigenous population and in certain cases engendered coloured, mixed-blood groups, as in South Africa and throughout Latin America. Since the boundaries of many ex-colonial states in Asia and Africa were artificially drawn for reasons of colonial expediency, they do not correspond to 'ethnic boundaries'. An ethnic group (for example, the Kurds) might be split among several states, or hitherto separate societies might be thrown together into a single deeply divided state (such as the Sudan). Within Europe, conquest and annexation were regular events until the 1950s.

New ethnic divisions are regularly formed as the result of involuntary population movements, including mass expulsions, flows of refugees, indentured or contracted labourers and large-scale enslavement. Armenians outside Turkey, Bengalis in India, Indians in East and Southern Africa and Blacks in the United States are several of the numerous cases. Free immigration also played a crucial role in the construction of ethnically split societies. The Americas and Australia were settled heavily by poor immigrants from Europe. They sought better economic and other opportunities and succeeded in forging new ethnic entities and identities.

In the post-World War II era, 'uneven development' has become a powerful push for the steady migration of the unemployed, the impoverished, or rather the relatively mobile in the developing countries, to the Western world. The flow of legal and illegal 'guest workers' to states such as the United States (mostly from Mexico), Israel (from the occupied territories) and Central and Western Europe (mostly from the Mediterranean countries) adds new ethnic groups and problems.

The rise of nationalism has stimulated the crystallization of ethnicity in many parts of the world. Nationalism is the claim of ethnic groups to self-determination. When an ethnic group achieves sovereignty in a certain state, it will become a nation which then excludes the other ethnic groups. The excluded ethnic groups are then forced to get organized and to seek a national minority status and an ethnic autonomy (Smith, 1981).

Diversity
The huge variety of formative processes make for enormous differences among ethnic groups on criteria of affiliation, relative size, geographical concentration, socio-economic standards,

political dominance, social separateness, identity, goals, collective consciousness and degree of organization.

One significant distinction is between race and ethnicity (van den Berghe, 1978). A racial group is composed of people who are believed to share the same biological make-up, while a non-racial ethnic group is identified by a cultural marker. Racial differentiation tends to be more visible, hierarchical, stigmatizing and mutually exclusive and allows less passing and mobility than non-racial differentiation. For this reason, subordinate racial groups like the Blacks in the United States tend to redefine their racial status in ethnic (cultural) terms. This is also why the South African government has switched recently from racial to ethnic terminology in presenting its *apartheid* policy.

A further fundamental distinction is between assimilating and non-assimilating ethnic (or racial) groups. The non-French immigrants to Canada, European immigrants to the United States and Jewish immigrants to Israel are predominantly assimilating ethnic groups. They wish and are allowed (or even pressured) to assimilate into the mainstream. On the other hand, in the same societies the French of Quebec, non-Whites in the United States and Arabs in Israel either insist on preserving their separate identity or are barred from assimilation. In due course assimilation reshapes ethnic boundaries and affiliations.

Yet dominance provides the best criterion to classify ethnic groups. There are certain societies where ethnic groups are more or less equal in their relative status and power. The Flemish and Walloons in Belgium, and the Germans, French and Italians in Switzerland are of this type. Most ethnic groups are, however, either dominant or subordinate. In such cases ethnic origin is embedded in the class and power structure of the society, producing an ethnic hierarchy. The extreme cases are the classic Indian caste system and the modern racial pyramid in South Africa. In an era when equality is spreading as an acceptable world norm, dominance is difficult to tolerate, and hence non-dominant ethnic groups tend to reject their subordinate position and to struggle for change.

Approaches

Social scientists disagree appreciably on the best way to conceive of ethnic groups. The debate hinges upon which of the defining characteristics of ethnicity is the most decisive: is it common descent, or rather shared culture or consciousness of kind? According to the 'ascriptive' (or 'primordialist') approach, members of an ethnic group are bound together by their common descent. Primary blood ties instil immutable emotional attachments and allegiances. Being 'given' and rigid, ethnicity transcends individual perceptions and changing circumstances. It is thus easier to activate people's sense of ethnic loyalty than their loyalty to such 'rational' organizations as trade unions.

The opposing view, known as the 'situational' ('subjectivist' or 'instrumental') approach, posits that what really matters is people's definition of themselves as culturally or physically distinct from others. Their shared descent is secondary and, if necessary, may be manufactured and manipulated (Cohen, 1974). Ethnicity is, therefore, flexible, adaptable and capable of taking different forms and meanings depending on the situation and perceptions of advantage. Consequently ethnic groups emerge, merge, and split constantly.

The contrast between the two viewpoints can be illustrated by asking, Who is a Palestinian? According to the ascriptive approach, all Arab inhabitants of Palestine until 1947 and their descendants were, are and will be Palestinians, regardless of their present place of residence, behaviours and attitudes. In contrast, the situational approach presents a much more complicated picture: up to the 1920s, the Palestinians were 'Syrian Arabs'; then, in the period up to the 1940s, they emerged as 'Palestinian *Arabs*'; during the 1950s and the 1960s they became 'Arab refugees'; and since the 1970s they have defined themselves as '*Palestinian* Arabs'. Second-generation Palestinians in the United States, Jordan and Israel differ in cultural traits, identity and manner from Palestinians in the West Bank, Gaza Strip and refugee camps. Further nuances in Palestinian identity and nationalism are generated by the differential and changing positions of significant outsiders – non-Palestinian Arabs, Israelis and others.

The situational view of ethnicity seems more valid and realistic. It is also in line with the shift in focus of the scientific study of ethnicity from a single ethnic group to *relations* between groups.

Sammy Smooha
University of Haifa

References

Cohen, A. (ed.) (1974), *Urban Ethnicity*, London.

Francis, E. K. (1976), *Interethnic Relations*, New York.

Smith, A. (1981), *The Ethnic Revival*, Cambridge.

Van den Berghe, P. L. (1978), *Race and Racism*, 2nd edn, New York.

Further Reading

Banton, M. (1967), *Race Relations*, London.

Mason, P. (1970), *Race Relations*, London.

van den Berghe, P. L. (1981), *The Ethnic Phenomenon*, New York.

See also: *ethnic relations*.

Ethnic Relations

Ethnic groups are groups which differ in descent, in cultural or physical traits, and in collective identity. The term 'ethnic relations' refers to the interactions between ethnic groups, relations that are very often replete with intolerance, hostility and violence.

The most common terms used to convey the troubled substance of ethnic relations are the social psychological concepts of prejudice and discrimination (Simpson and Yinger, 1971). 'Prejudice' is a set of preconceived rigid beliefs, emotions and preferences of one ethnic group towards another (for example, the idea that all Blacks are lazy), whereas 'discrimination' is a denial of equal treatment on ethnic grounds (thus, refusing a person a job for being Black). It is thus assumed that if prejudice and discrimination were eliminated, relations between the ethnic groups would cease to be problematic.

These concepts have proved, however, to be of limited value in understanding ethnic relations. It has become clear, for instance, that the present Black-White inequality in occupational achievements in the United States would not vanish if White Americans as individuals start to think of and treat Blacks and Whites in the same way. Neither could one adequately describe or explain the Nazi holocaust in terms of prejudicial beliefs and discriminatory actions of German individuals.

To overcome such difficulties, it is necessary to shift to *institutional terms*, such as ethnic ideology and institutional discrimination. 'Ethnic ideology' is a system of beliefs regarding existing and desirable ethnic relations. Nationalism, racism, Nazism, *apartheid*, assimilation and cultural pluralism are important ethnic ideologies that are institutionalized in certain countries, transmitted through the media, schools, churches, and families, made into state policies, and allocated appreciable resources for implementation. They are much more consequential for ethnic relations than individual prejudices.

Similarly, discrimination is more effective in its institutional than in its personal form. Institutional discrimination is evident when the normal functioning, whether intended or not, of a given institution (such as education or the economy) results in the unequal distribution of benefits or deprivations to different ethnic groups. For instance, when unemployment disproportionately hits the lower classes in which Blacks are over-represented, one may talk of institutional discrimination regardless of whether economic policy makers are aware of it or not (Wilson, 1978).

Institutional analysis, which is made possible by these broader concepts, is superior to interpersonal analysis because it treats ethnic relations as part of the structure and processes of the whole society and not in terms of individual responses. Ethnic relations are not determined by the irrational behaviours, ignorance and bigotry of some 'bad' people, but rather constitute a system of institutionalized behaviour, norms, sanctions, organizations, vested interests, tensions, conflicts, and so on evolving from fairly continuous contacts between ethnic groups.

Main Types of Ethnic Relations

Although ethnic relations take a wide variety of forms, the major ones are: (1) assimilation, (2) consociationalism, (3) domination and other, mostly mixed or transient, situations.

(1) In assimilationist situations, ethnic groups merge by adopting common cultural patterns, sharing the same institutions, intermarrying, and eventually they lose their distinctiveness. States which allow or push (but do not impose by force) assimilation are quite tolerant. They tend (a) to incorporate ethnic members as equal citizens, making little or no ethnic distinction in their laws or practices, and (b) to have a multi-ethnic élite or at least an élite fairly open to members of the subordinate groups. Universalistic treatment makes ethnic solidarity redundant; open élite structure legitimizes the ethnic status quo, and both encourage ethnic assimilation.

Assimilation rarely takes the form of a true melting pot which produces a genuinely new nation. Mexico is one of these extraordinary cases where the Spanish, Indians and Blacks were amalgamated to such an extent that a new mestizo Mexican culture, people, and identity emerged, to which each constituent group made a recognizable contribution. More commonly, the subordinate group assimilates into the dominant group. Van den Berghe (1981) characterizes the group most likely to assimilate as follows: 'An immigrant group similar in physical appearance and culture to the group to which it assimilates, smaller in proportion to the total population, of low status and territorially dispersed.' This profile applies to the 32 million immigrants from Europe to the United States during 1820–1930 who were largely assimilated into the Anglo-Saxon mainstream. Assimilation also succeeded because it was a common goal and a channel of social mobility for the poor European immigrants.

Assimilation in Mexico and the United States has not phased ethnicity out entirely but rather reduced it to such a level that it no longer regulates everyday life. Nor does it shape such cardinal decisions as which job to enter and whom to marry. As Gans (1979) puts it, 'real' immigrant ethnicity was so diluted over generations as to become 'symbolic' only.

At the same time it should be emphasized that Anglo-Saxon qualities in the United States and Spanish features in Mexico have remained the most cherished values and continue to figure significantly in status attainment.

(2) The course of ethnic relations is quite different in 'consociational' states such as Switzerland, Canada, Belgium, Austria, Yugoslavia, Nigeria and Lebanon (Lijphart, 1977). Far from assimilating, ethnic groups in these states keep their distinct cultures, institutions and identities and interact on a more or less equal footing ('consociationalism' literally means 'association between equals'). They are politically organized, and a mechanism for their proportional representation in key positions is set up. Their élites that join together to form the national élite are intensively engaged in the politics of accommodation and bargaining. Since every constituent ethnic group has a veto power on questions of vital interest to it, no decision can be made unless consensus is reached, a situation that quite often leads to a deadlock. While the vested interests of every group are carefully guarded, conflicts are difficult to resolve and problems are not satisfactorily settled. The largest or most powerful group has no choice but to share proportionately resources and decisions with the other ethnic groups which are unassimilable but sufficiently powerful to disrupt the system if they are not accorded their due share. Hence, consociationalism evolves as a compromise or parity situation when none of the other options – assimilation, domination and total separation – is feasible.

The contrast between Switzerland and Lebanon demonstrates the strengths and weaknesses of consociationalism. In Switzerland the division into predominantly homogeneous cantons enables each of the three major linguistic groups to exercise full cultural and territorial autonomy, while the federal institutions supply a shared framework with proportional representation, and the internationally recognized neutrality insulates the system from external pressures. This successful

Swiss consociational democracy emerged and developed gradually over the last seven centuries.

Lebanon, in contrast, failed to develop the essential national consensus over its identity as a separate Arab state, without a Moslem dominant majority, and without being a party to the Israeli-Arab conflict. Proportional representation, which is the core of consociationalism, also became controversial as a result of the shifting demographic ratios and the rise of traditionally undeveloped groups (for example, the Shi'ites). Furthermore, the Lebanese did not enjoy the time and freedom available to the Swiss to work out their internal problems; they were instead continuously subjected to foreign rule or interventions. Indeed, the civil war in 1975 was the direct outcome of the crucial role played by non-Lebanese (the Palestinians, Syrians and Israelis).

(3) *Dominant* patterns of ethnic relations are more commonly found. Here one ethnic group clearly controls the other ethnic groups, monopolizes decision making, establishes its own culture as the prevalent one, appropriates to itself the lion's share of resources, and exacts from the subordinate groups various services and benefits. Compliance is achieved by a series of measures, including economic dependence, political regulation, élite co-optation and segregation, that decrease the subordinate groups' capacity to resist. Domination may be made acceptable to the subordinate groups as the price of living in a stable society and receiving protection against persecution, deportation and bloodshed.

Dominance appears in many variations, the most important being slavery, indentured labour, caste systems, conquest, empires, colonialism, and their legacies in modern states such as South Africa and Israel (for Arabs). The most relevant brand of slavery, for instance, is 'chattel slavery', which prevailed in the New World. It was, indeed, a dominant pattern of race relations where Whites controlled Blacks, exploited them economically and sexually, deprived them of human rights, atomized them to the extent that they could not build a community and resist, and let them absorb their masters' culture but not assimilate. Slavery was accompanied by racism in the United

States, but was much less racist in Latin America where Blacks, to a large extent, penetrated into and assimilated to the dominant White group.

After the demise of colonialism all over the world and especially in Black Africa, the rule of the White minority in South Africa stands out as the most blatant contemporary modern system of domination (Adam and Giliomee, 1979). The prospects for democratization in the foreseeable future are slim because of the following combination of conditions: (a) since Whites feel as native as the Africans do and regard South Africa as their only homeland, they will not depart, as did White settlers elsewhere; (b) Whites depend on non-White labour for their exceedingly high standard of living; (c) the liberal alternatives of assimilation, majority rule, consociational democracy, or negotiated partition are less advantageous for Whites than the status quo, and (d) Whites are strong enough to withstand internal unrest and external pressures. To sustain White domination, the South African government removed, in the late 1970s, superfluous economic and segregationist restrictions.

There are other situations which do not fit neatly into any of the above three patterns. One is the warfare frontier setting involving the large-scale liquidation of the widely dispersed and 'useless' natives by the technologically superior overseas settlers (for example, the Aborigines in Australia, the Indians in the Americas). The number of transient and mixed situations in our era of rapid change is also increasing. Cases in point are Black-White relations in the United States and the Catholic-Protestant relations in Northern Ireland, both following the collapse of domination in the 1960s.

Approaches to the Study of Ethnic Relations
Three major approaches have emerged in the social sciences to account for the tremendous variation in ethnic relations, particularly in industrial societies: the (1) cultural, (2) class and (3) pluralist.

(1) The cultural perspective sees cultural differences as the prime factor shaping ethnic relations. Modernization and the

building of national institutions such as mass media, schools, political parties, industrial plants and trade unions gradually replace the ethnic traditional cultural and primordial ties by new overarching values and identities. Greater ethnic equality and assimilation will also result from modernization. This school of thought takes the Western experience as a model for other countries, forecasting the decline of ethnicity in the long run despite temporary digressions (Deutsch, 1966; Eisenstadt and Stein, 1973).

(2) The class theorists, on the other hand, expect rather a continuous revival of ethnicity caused by the exacerbation of internal contradictions in the world capitalist economy (Bonacich, 1980; Wallerstein, 1979). They regard contemporary ethnic situations as by-products of capitalism which necessitated large-scale population movements (slaves, indentured labourers, guest workers, poor immigrants), colonialism (colonies as economic enterprises) and imperialism (cheap raw materials, new markets). The subordinate groups suffer from both class and ethnic deprivation, but they are slowly rising to liberate themselves from dependence, economic exploitation and ethnic discrimination.

(3) In contrast to the cultural and class approaches, the pluralist one assumes no *a priori* universal factor or trend in ethnic relations. (Kuper and Smith, 1969; van den Berghe, 1973). It rather takes the vast diversity of ethnic relations as its vantage point, claiming that the dynamics vary appreciably from one situation to another. Thus the main determinant of ethnic relations is ethnicity in Black Africa, as compared to class in Latin America (van den Berghe, 1981). The pluralists also deny that Western development necessarily leads to assimilation or to non-ethnic liberal democracy, and point to a number of Western consociational democracies in which ethnicity is institutionalized, and to the spread of ethnic strife in some Western countries (Esman, 1977). Modernization may have various consequences for ethnicity, depending on other features of the ethnic situation (for example, industrialization encouraged the assimilation of European immigrants but not Blacks in the United States).

Strategies of Change

Policy makers and social scientists are hard pressed to formulate strategies to tackle the mounting ethnic problems. One general strategy is to ensure equality of rights and to create opportunities for contact between ethnic groups. The United Nations adopted several declarations on these lines, and many states enacted laws whose aim was to provide individual members of different ethnic groups with equal rights and protection against discrimination. Prejudice is combated through dissemination of information on minorities and the overall upgrading of the educational standard of the general population. Intergroup contact in schools, workplaces, armed forces and in experimental settings has also been used to promote ethnic tolerance (Katz, 1976).

While such a strategy is geared to removing barriers to assimilation, a competing strategy is to improve the conditions conducive for the retention and equalization of ethnic groups. Some of these measures include provision of ethnic group rights, cultural and territorial autonomy, and the extension of the principle of proportional representation to various posts and benefits. Most of them are embodied in the constitution or structure of many multi-ethnic states with federal or confederal structures. The idea is that through these measures, systems of ethnic domination can be transformed into consociational democracies.

The cases of Northern Ireland and South Africa reveal the difficulties inherent in the process. The British programme to resolve the ethnic dispute in Northern Ireland through power-sharing was blocked in the mid-1970s by the Protestant majority. More calculating and hesitant is the government of South Africa's attempt to harness consociational arrangements for alleviating its racial tensions. In the early 1980s it proposed a constitutional reform aptly branded by critics 'sham consociationalism', that aimed to broaden its racial base by co-opting the Coloureds and Asians into the White system (Hanf, Weiland and Vierdag, 1981).

A radical strategy is to reduce or eliminate ethnic relations by territorial and physical means. One possibility is secession or partition, like the successive divisions of the Indian sub-continent into India, Pakistan and Bangladesh. Another related method calls for population transfers, successfully completed in the early 1920s between Turkey, Greece and Bulgaria. The extremist variations – which are by no means infrequent – are mass deportations and genocidal attempts (Kuper, 1981). Peaceful reconstitution of state boundaries and voluntary population exchanges are not generally a practical solution, however, because they would require, in view of the present ethnic mess, a virtual revamping of the world political map and immense population movements.

Ethnic problems will endure, and, like all other social problems, there are no overall stock solutions. What could be more realistically expected is some reduction in ethnic conflict if the principle of negotiated conflict regulation gains greater acceptance.

Sammy Smooha
University of Haifa

References

Adam, H. and Giliomee, H. (1979), *Ethnic Power Mobilized*, New Haven.

Bonacich, E. (1980), 'Class approaches to ethnicity and race', *The Insurgent Sociologist*, 10.

Deutsch, K. W. (1966), *Nationalism and Social Communication*, Cambridge, Mass.

Eisenstadt, S. N. and Stein, R. (eds) (1973), *Building States and Nations*, Beverly Hills.

Esman, M. J. (ed.) (1977), *Ethnic Conflict in the Western World*, Ithaca.

Gans, H. J. (1979), 'Symbolic ethnicity: the future of ethnic groups and cultures in America', *Ethnic and Racial Studies*, 2.

Hanf, Th., Weiland, H. and Vierdag, G. (1981), *South Africa: The Prospects for Peaceful Change*, London.

Katz, P. A. (ed.) (1976), *Towards the Elimination of Racism*, New York.

Kuper, L. (1981), *Genocide*, Harmondsworth.

Kuper, L. and Smith, M. G. (eds) (1969), *Pluralism in Africa*, Berkeley and Los Angeles.

Lijphart, A. (1977), *Democracy in Plural Societies*, New Haven.

Simpson, G. E. and Yinger, J. M. (1972), *Racial and Ethnic Minorities*, New York.

Van den Berghe, P. L. (1973), 'Pluralism', in J. J. Honigman (ed.), *Handbook for Social and Cultural Anthropology*, Chicago.

Van den Berghe, P. L. (1981), *The Ethnic Phenomenon*, New York.

Wallerstein, E. (1979), *The Capitalist World-Economy*, Cambridge.

Wilson, W. J. (1978), *The Declining Significance of Race*, Chicago.

Further Reading

Glazer, N. and Moynihan, D. P. (eds) (1975), *Ethnicity: Theory and Experience*, Cambridge, Mass.

Hechter, M. (1975), *Internal Colonialism*, London.

Rex, J. (1970), *Race Relations in Sociological Theory*, London.

See also: *ethnic groups; prejudice.*

Gangs

The term gang is at once commonplace and controversial. It is necessary to distinguish gangs and subcultures, on the one hand, and gangs and youth groups, on the other. Reduced to the simplest terms, (youth) gangs are *non-adult sponsored adolescent groups*, that is, groups whose members meet together somewhat regularly, and over time, on the basis of *self-defined* criteria of membership and with some sense of territoriality (Miller, 1974). It is improper to include *behaviour* in defining gangs, for that is often what we wish to explain or understand. Similarly, organizational characteristics do not define gangs, for these vary among gangs as among other youth groups.

Territoriality is important in defining gangs and in explaining differences between gangs, as well as other youth collectivities. Identification with a 'hanging' or 'ranging' *area* typifies gangs, while adult-sponsored groups typically identify with an institution, such as a school, church, or agency. In any case, the adult world context is important. In Northern Ireland, for example, the Catholic-Protestant conflict has intruded on the traditional, territorially-based identity of some youth gangs.

Subcultures are shared systems of values, artifacts, and reference, among individuals and groups. The existence of a local gang culture is indicated, for example, when younger boys (and girls) aspire to become members of a local gang. In general, however, age grading is not so rigid – nor are age distinctions so fine – among gangs as among other youth groups, especially those that are adult-sponsored. When rivalries develop between gangs, the subculture may take on a *conflict* character with implications for gang organization (roles, performance criteria, valued artifacts and skills). Gang subcultures emerge from interaction within and between groups, and between groups and institutions of the larger society, such as police, schools, the economic sector (Short, 1974).

Most members of even the most delinquent gang are not delinquent most of the time. Typically, a few members will take part in any given delinquency episode, while most do not. Delinquent episodes may erupt when a gang leader's status, or the status of an entire gang, is challenged or threatened. What is considered threatening varies among gangs with differing subcultural orientations.

Delinquency committed by gangs may be very serious, yet most often it is trivial. Gangs are responsible for much serious crime in some localities, but for most gang members, violence and other serious crime is rare and quite incidental.

The existence and continuity of a gang may be determined by forces external to the gang. Paradoxically, the youth-oriented quality of troublesome gangs results from the exclusion of young people from large areas of adult institutional life. Social separation produces cultural differentiation, and when separation is categorical – based on categories such as age, sex, race, ethnicity, or class – subcultural differentiation is likely to develop along these lines. Persons who share the characteristics which are the basis of separation develop their own status systems, beliefs, and ways of meeting problems among themselves and in relationships with the rest of the world.

James F. Short, Jr
Washington State University

References
Miller, W. B. (1974), 'American youth gangs: past and present', in A. S. Blumberg (ed.), *Current Perspectives on Criminal Behavior: Original Essays on Criminology*, New York.
Short, J. F., Jr (1974), 'Collective behavior, crime, and delinquency', in D. Glaser (ed.), *Handbook of Criminology*, Chicago.
See also: *subculture*.

Gerontology, Social

Gerontology is the scientific study of biological, psychological and sociocultural aspects of the ageing process. Social gerontology is concerned only with its sociological-anthropological component. Although public interest in old age commonly stems from the association of ageing with 'social problems', such considerations will be excluded from the present discussion.

Social gerontology emerged in the late 1950s, and has become established as a recognized subject of study and research in academic institutes throughout the world, most especially in the United States. The conceptual approaches and methodologies applied in this new field reflect a wide gamut of theoretical frameworks and techniques. None the less, three core issues in the study of behavioural phenomena in later life can be identified: (1) the relative importance in ageing of universal human processes and specific cultural factors; (2) the dialectic between stability and change in later life; (3) questions concerning the place of the elderly in a social structure, and in the symbolic worlds of both the aged and non-aged.

(1) The quest for universal, generic characteristics of ageing has taken several theoretical forms. Some anthropologists have imputed common needs and aspirations to all old people, such as the desire for a prolonged life and dignified death, and they

have tried to identify general role features, such as a shift from active participation in economic production to sedentary advisory roles. Similarly, 'disengagement theory' states that there is a gradual process of mutual disengagement between the aged person and his society in all cultures. Critics have cited cross-cultural and cross-sectional data to show that there have been a variety of context-bound, behavioural responses to old age. It has also been argued that patterns of active behaviour among the elderly, as well as manifestations of retreatism and inertia, are conditioned by environmental constraints and cultural configurations. More recently, however, some psychologists with a similar universalist bias have maintained that the process of ageing is governed by an increased concentration on the inner self, and especially on a retrospective life-review.

(2) Ageing is a dynamic process of concurrent transformations in various spheres of life. In a complex, changing society, where life transitions are generally equated with social mobility and progress within a given career opportunity structure, the changes associated with old age engender a paradoxical perception of later life. In a social structure which allocates statuses and prestige according to mastery of information, control of wealth and command of physical resources and mental faculties, the aged are conceived of as a stagnant, marginal social category. This stereotype persists, in spite of the growing numbers of elderly persons whose life expectancy is increasing and whose functioning capacities are improving relative to previous generations. Such incongruity between social definition and personal experience generates ambivalence and ambiguity. In the experience of the temporal universe of the aged, long-term planning becomes problematic, if not impossible. The past is recalled selectively, and is mined in order to construct a meaningful present. The struggle of old people for continuity in identity is often expressed through their review and reinterpretation of life-histories, as well as through their reorganization of social relationships and systems of meaning. Temporal asynchrony and disorganization of this kind usually does not exist in so-called simple societies, where the position of the aged accurately reflects the balance between their control of valuable resources

and their diminishing ability to protect their interests. In some economically 'hand-to-mouth' preliterate societies, an aged person whose presence becomes a burden may be abandoned, or ritually killed. In agricultural societies, however, knowledge and spiritual powers are attributed to the aged. Elders have social and ritual roles entailing a honourable place in society.

(3) Social roles are often associated with age categories. Passage through a series of age grades represents an important organizing principle of social life in most simple societies. In modern societies, age is less significant than occupational specialization. Yet the phases of 'childhood' and 'old age' are, by definition, social categories circumscribed by age norms, which are decisive in shaping individuals' social identities. The very fact that age alone is enough to define the 'old' reflects the disappearance of the normally decisive occupational and other roles and values, which in turn generates negative images and stereotypes of the elderly. This phenomenon has led a number of scholars to consider the potential development of subcultural or countercultural social units made up exclusively of the aged. Research on such groups, mainly in age-homogeneous communities, day centres and residential settings, shows that in many cases a new alternative system of social relationships and symbolic meanings is developed to supersede those of the prior, stigmatizing and alienating social milieu.

Social gerontology is currently in a transitional phase. Many aspects of ageing can be analysed and explained by other disciplines, but the growing reservoir of data and theory on old age encourages social research into such specific issues as the politics of ageing, ageing and the law, and the existential problems connected with old age. Much research is also directed to the aged as a 'social problem' and the object of public social concern. The central problems have been defined, but there is as yet no adequate theoretical treatment of them.

Haim Hazan
Tel-Aviv University

Further Reading

Binstock, R. H. and Shanes, E. (eds) (1976), *Handbook of Aging and the Social Sciences*, New York.

Hareven, T. K. and Adams, K. J. (eds) (1982), *Ageing and Life Course Transitions*, London.

Holmes, L. (1983), *Other Culture, Elder Years*, St Paul.

Myerhoff, B. G. and Simic, A. (eds) (1978), *Life's Career and Aging: Cultural Variations on Growing Old*, Beverly Hills.

See also: *ageing*.

Homosexuality

Although same-sex erotic experiences exist across cultures and throughout history with varying degrees of acceptability and frequency, it was not until the nineteenth century in Europe and America that homosexuality was invented as an object of scientific investigation. The term itself was introduced by a sympathetic Hungarian doctor, Benkert, in 1869 amidst a flurry of attempts at classifying sexuality (Ulrich's term 'Uranians' indicating a kind of third sex was popular, as was the concept of 'invert'). From this time until the 1970s, the dominant mode of thinking about homosexuality was clinical – it was primarily viewed as a pathology, its causes were located in biological degeneracy or family pathology, and treatments, ranging from castration to psychoanalysis, were advocated. Although such an approach continues (for example in the work of Socarides, 1978), since 1973 the American Psychiatric Association has officially removed homosexuality from its clinical nomenclature, seeing it as nonpathological in itself (Bayer, 1981). Ironically, some of the leading clinicians, and notably Freud, had never viewed it as a pathology: in 1935 Freud could write in a famous 'letter to a mother' that whilst 'homosexuality is assuredly no advantage, it is nothing to be classified as an illness; we consider it to be a variation of the sexual development . . .'

While the nineteenth century saw the ascendancy of the clinical model of homsexuality, it also saw the growth of writing and campaigning which challenged the orthodox heterosexual assumptions. Thus Magnus Hirschfield established the Scientific Humanitarian Committee and the Institute for Sexual

Science in Germany in 1897 and campaigned through scientific research for the acceptance of homosexuality up until the 1930s, when the Nazi movement stopped such advocacies and started a policy of extermination instead. Others, such as Carpenter in England and Gide in France, pursued a more literary defence (Lauritsen and Thorstad, 1974). It was not, however, until the period after the Second World War that a substantial body of published research suggested the ubiquity and normality of homosexual experience. Pivotal to this enterprise was the publication of the Kinsey Report in 1948 and 1953 containing the findings of interviews with well over 12,000 American men and women. Amongst the former, Kinsey found that 37 per cent had some post-adolescent homosexual orgasm and 4 per cent had a preponderance of such experience; amongst the latter, the figures were around 13 per cent and 3 per cent respectively. When Kinsey added that such responses were to be found amongst all social groups and in all walks of life, he created a social bombshell; when he concluded that homosexual behaviour was neither unnatural nor neurotic in itself but an 'inherent physiologic capacity', he established an outrageous view that was later to be turned into something of an orthodoxy in the research of others like Hooker in America and Schofield in England (Freedman, 1971).

Throughout this period, however, homosexuality was strongly condemned by law in most European countries and in all American states. It was not until the 1960s – and a decade or so after proposals for change in the British Wolfenden report and the American New Model Code – that the legal situation changed. (See Crane, 1982, for the current legal situation.) Despite the progressive build-up of homosexual groups during the 1950s, it is the New York 'Stonewall Riots' of 1969 which are generally taken to symbolize the birth of the modern international 'Gay Movement' (Weeks, 1977; D'Emilio, 1983). The scientifically imposed term 'homosexual' was shifted to the self-created one 'gay'; medical rhetoric was converted to political language; organizations for gays became widespread in most large cities, and millions of gay men and women started to 'come out' and identify positively with the term 'gay'. The

1970s therefore demonstrated a real change in gay experiences – a change well documented in Dennis Altman's *The Homosexualisation of America and the Americanisation of the Homosexual* (1982).

All of this has left its impact upon research. Although there are still those who study causes and cures, it is noticeable that social scientists have largely left this question behind and turned to new areas. Thus, the history of homosexuality has started to be unearthed in much the same ways as women's history has been explored by feminist social scientists. This has meant not just the discovery of the documents of the recent past – as in Katz's *Gay American History* (1976) – but also excavations into the more distant past such as ancient Greece (Dover, 1978), the Middle Ages (Boswell, 1980) and the Renaissance (Faderman, 1981). Far from being universally condemned, homosexual experiences have been reacted to in very different ways throughout history, and indeed, have been experienced as something very different at different times. Closely related to this historical research has been a concern to understand why groups and societies have condemned same-sex experience and how such stigmatizing perceptions have had a profound and sometimes negative impact upon them. This has meant that some social psychologist have turned to the analysis of 'homophobia' – the morbid fear of homosexuals (Weinberg, 1972) – some have been interested in studying the labelling of homosexuality (Plummer, 1981), whilst still others have seen homosexuality as constituted by a discourse which embodies power relationships (Foucault, 1979).

Another significant shift in research interests has developed from modern feminism. Arguing that lesbianism should be approached within the framework of women's studies rather than that of male homosexuality, it has directed attention to concerns like child custody problems and the growth of political lesbianism as an explicit rejection of male sexuality (see Ettore, 1980).

Perhaps the most significant change in research has been the sheer range of studies to show the diversity of homosexual experience. The noun 'homosexual' has been replaced by the term 'homosexualities' to signpost as much diversity as is found behind the label 'heterosexual' – there are many ways of becoming gay, and there are many ways of being gay. Amongst these concerns are such features as the different age structures (from being a child to being 'gray and gay'); the different relationships (from gay couples and gay parents to elaborate friendship networks); the different institutions (from gay 'pick-up' places to gay counselling), and the different life cycles that surround gayness (most notably the problems of 'coming out' and choosing a particular lifestyle (Levine, 1979)). These studies, perhaps more than any others, have indicated the full range of humanity behind the straitjacketing label of homosexuality.

Ken Plummer
University of Essex

References
Altman, D. (1982), *The Homosexualisation of America and the Americanisation of the Homosexual*, New York.
Bayer, R. (1981), *Homosexuality and American Psychiatry: The Politics of Diagnosis*, New York.
Boswell, J. (1980), *Christianity, Social Tolerance and Homosexuality*, Chicago.
Crane, P. (1982), *Gays and the Law*, London.
D'Emilio, J. (1983) *Sexual Politics, Sexual Communities: The Making of a Homosexual Minority in the United States, 1940–1970*, Chicago.
Dover, K. (1978), *Greek Homosexuality*, London.
Ettore, E. (1980), *Lesbians, Women and Society*, London.
Faderman, L. (1981), *Surpassing the Love of Men: Romantic Friendships among Women from the Renaissance to the Present Day*, London.
Foucault, M. (1979), *The History of Sexuality: Vol. 1 –An Introduction*, London.
Freedman, M. (1971), *Homosexuality and Psychological Functioning*, California.
Katz, J. (1976), *Gay American History: Lesbians and Gay Men in the U.S.A.*, New York.

Lauritsen, J. and Thorstad, D. (1974), *The Early Homosexual Rights Movement* (1864–1935), New York.

Levine, M. P. (ed.) (1979), *Gay Men: The Sociology of Male Homosexuality*, New York.

Plummer, K. (ed.) (1981), *The Making of the Modern Homosexual*, London.

Socarides, C. (1978), *Homosexuality*, New York.

Weeks, J. (1977), *Coming Out: Homosexual Politics in Britain from the 19th Century to the Present*, London.

Weinberg, G. (1972), *Society and the Healthy Homosexual*, New York.

Incest Behaviour

Most writings on incest by social scientists deal with theoretical aspects of incest avoidance and prohibition, while neglecting the incidence and implications of the act itself. The two issues are obviously related but not identical, and a complete grasp of the problem requires an integrated understanding of both phenomena which is presently lacking.

The classic approach to the prohibition question has been to assume that, at some unspecified point in the past, human beings instituted a rule against intrafamilial sex, and hence marriage, in recognition of the potential biological, social and/or psychological effects of inbreeding. Such an argument, which has been espoused by Freud (1950) and most past and present social scientists, implies that humans have an inclination toward incest which is constrained by explicit rules. The lack of historical evidence for the actual institutionalization of such a prohibition, and the absence of an explicit injunction against incest in many societies which nevertheless do not condone it, has argued against this approach. In contrast, Edward Westermarck (1926) argued that human beings evolved with an avoidance of incest; some societies then promulgated rules which supported this inclination. For supporters of this notion, this would explain why inbreeding has never been the pattern for any society, including those without apparent rules against it. Circumstantial evidence from natural ethnographic settings which prevailed in traditional China (Wolf and Huang,

1980) and on contemporary Israeli *kibbutzim* (Shepher, 1971) has been interpreted as support for the conclusion that humans tend to avoid sexual contact with people with whom they have been raised in close contact from early childhood. Moreover, animal ethologists have demonstrated that all non-human primate species tend to avoid inbreeding by a variety of social arrangements. Thus, the position that mankind evolved with what is also a biologically advantageous impulsion to outbreed has gained ascendancy in recent years. Today, adherents of such a view disagree on whether or not such a pattern is genetically programmed, or the result of behavioural imprinting or negative reinforcement at an early age.

A major problem of this sociobiological approach, as with the preceding cultural one, is accounting for why incest itself takes place in both Western and some non-Western societies, In response, Robin Fox (1962) has suggested that in some societies, including our own, household arrangements and the socialization process, which involve a lack of physical contact among siblings when young, lead both to availability and attraction when they reach sexual maturity. This, he argues, would account for both the prohibition against and the incidence of incestuous contacts. An implication of this argument is that cultural arrangements can either fail to produce or fail to overcome natural tendencies to avoid sexual relations among those reared together.

The existence of institutionalized incest, in the form of father/daughter or, more commonly, brother/sister marriage among royalty in a variety of ancient states, including Egypt, Peru, Persia, Thailand, Hawaii, Japan, and possibly many others, presents another problem with the avoidance theory. Moreover. it has been recently suggested that, during the three centuries of Roman rule in Egypt, incestuous marriages were also prevalent among the propertied middle class (Hopkins, 1980). Sociobiologists have taken the position that the royal marriages can be explained in terms of the concept of 'inclusive fitness', that is, they are a means of ensuring the maximum chance of continuity of one's genes into the next generation. This interpretation is undermined by the erroneous historical assumption that such marriages had reproduction as their practical end. This was not the case, even for the oft-cited example of Cleopatra, who was not an offspring of her father's marriage to his sister (Bixler, 1982). Marriages of this sort had cultural strategies related to indigenous perceptions of the nature of royalty and the right to rule, rather than reproductive ones. None the less, these unions, as well as the yet not fully understood case of Egyptian middle-class marriages, suggest, as is also the case for noninstitutionalized incest, that cultural conditions can generate incest in different contexts and for different purposes. This also implies that if there is a sociobiological basis for incest avoidance, then the subsequent evolution of the human capacity for cultural innovation overcomes this inherent inclination. In other words, the human species may be responsible for creating the concept of incest and its practice, rather than the prohibition. Evaluating such a proposition will require a more detailed and systematic study of incest in its various forms.

W. Arens
State University of New York
Stony Brook

References

Bixler, R. (1982), 'Sibling incest in the royal families of Egypt, Peru, and Hawaii', *The Journal of Sex Research*, 18.

Fox, R. (1962), 'Sibling incest', *British Journal of Sociology*, 13.

Freud, S. (1950), *Totem and Taboo*, New York.

Hopkins, R. (1980), 'Brother-sister marriage in Roman Egypt', *Comparative Studies in Society and History*, 22.

Shepher, J. (1971), 'Mate selection among second generation kibbutz adolescents and adults', *Archives of Sexual Behaviour*, 1.

Westermarck, E. (1926), *A Short History of Human Marriage*, London.

Wolf, A. and Huang, C. (1980), *Marriage and Adoption in China, 1845–1945*, Stanford, California.

Further Reading
Arens, W. (1985), *The Original Sin*, New York.
Shepher, J. (1983), *Incest: A Biosocial View*, New York.

Labelling Theory

Durkheim declared of criminal activities that 'what confers this character upon them is not the intrinsic quality of a given act but the definition which the collective consciousness lends them' (1938 [1895]; see Becker, 1973). Most labelling theorists, however, trace their intellectual lineage to G. H. Mead (1928), although his ideas about societal definition of crime are not very different from Durkheim's. In 1931, Shaw entitled his first chapter about a delinquent, 'Labelling a Moron', but his intention was to indicate how delinquents are *mislabelled*.

The Chicago School of Sociology, of which Mead and Shaw were members, stimulated numerous studies of both the structural and interactional aspects of deviance. In Tannenbaum's (1938) study, data and analysis combined to produce the first major example of modern labelling theory. He argued that a young person's leisure activities are given opposite 'definitions of the situation' by the actor and his community. For the former, they constitute play, adventure, excitement, and so on; for the latter, they are evil. Gradually there is a shift from the definition of specific acts as evil to the definition or 'tagging' of the actor himself as evil. The actor accepts this classification and, in the company of a gang of youths similarly classified, behaves accordingly. The idea that societal reaction to deviance worsens matters was taken up by Wilkins (1964), with his concept of 'deviance amplification', while Lemert (1967) propounded the famous dictum, 'Older sociology tended to rest heavily upon the idea that deviance leads to social control. I have come to believe that the reverse idea, i.e., social control leads to deviance, is equally tenable and the potentially richer premise for studying deviance in modern society.'

The development of labelling theory has had an impact on research. Schur (1964) hypothesized that a heroin subculture was less prominent in Britain than in America, because America stamped addicts as criminals, forcing them to resort to crime, rather than physicians, in order to obtain supplies. Cohen (1972) noted how insignificant battles between 'mods' and 'rockers' were exaggerated by the media, causing other young people to seek publicity and reputation by identifying themselves as members of these groups.

Conventional criminologists denied that deviance as a consequence of societal reaction was significant. 'Radical' criminologists also attacked labelling theory, remonstrating that it distracted attention from the capitalist system, which created criminal conditions in the first place. In response, Becker (1973) discarded the term labelling, of which he had been the main disseminator, declaring himself in the mainstream of interactionist theory, which, he argued, in no way ruled out analysis of the interaction between the powerful and the oppressed.

The present state of labelling theory is confused. One group of statistical criminologists (Gove, 1975) claims to have disproved the existence of labelling effects, whereas another such group (West and Farrington, 1977) claims the opposite. Ericson (1975) and Ditton (1979) cogently suggest that more precise identification of the various mechanisms which might lie behind labelling effects is called for, rather than merely iterating rejoinders (for example Downes and Rock, 1979) to denunciatory critics.

Maurice Glickman
University of Botswana

References
Becker, H. (1973), *Outsiders: Studies in the Sociology of Deviance*, 2nd edn, London.
Cohen, S. (1972), *Folk Devils and Moral Panics: The Creation of the Mods and Rockers*, London.
Ditton, J. (1979), *Controlology: Beyond the New Criminology*, London.
Downes, D. and Rock, P. (eds) (1979), *Deviant Interpretations*, Oxford.
Durkheim, E. (1938 [1895]), *The Rules of Sociological Method*,

London. (Original French edn, *Les Règles de la méthode sociologique*, Paris.)

Ericson, R. (1975), *Criminal Reactions: The Labelling Perspective*, Farnborough.

Gove, W. (ed.) (1975), *The Labelling of Deviance*, London.

Lemert, E. (1967), *Human Deviance, Social Problems and Social Control*, Englewood Cliffs, N.J.

Mead, G. H. (1928), 'The psychology of punitive justice', *American Sociological Review*, 23.

Schur, E. (1964), 'Drug addiction under British policy', in H. Becker (ed.), *The Other Side: Perspectives on Deviance*, London.

Shaw, C. (1931), *The Natural History of a Delinquent Career*, Chicago.

Tannenbaum, F. (1938), *Crime and the Community*, New York.

West, D. and Farrington, D. (1977), *The Delinquent Way of Life*, London.

Wilkins, L. (1964), *Social Deviance*, London.

See also: *deviance*.

Loneliness

Loneliness can range from fleeting moods to severe and chronic states; it is the more extreme forms of loneliness that concern social scientists and the general public. A distinction can be made between emotional loneliness that occurs when an individual lacks an intimate relationship with one special person such as a spouse or parent, and social loneliness that occurs when an individual lacks friends or has no sense of belonging to a community (Rubenstein and Shaver, 1982; Weiss, 1973).

It is useful to distinguish loneliness from other, related, concepts. Loneliness is a subjective experience that is not identical to objective social isolation. Solitude is not invariably accompanied by loneliness. Although lonely people often report having fewer social ties than the non-lonely, many exceptions to this pattern occur. It is also useful to distinguish the psychological loneliness studied by most researchers from the philosophical concept of existential loneliness. From the existential view, loneliness refers to an individual's awareness that we are ultimately separate from others and must confront life challenges on our own (Moustakas, 1972).

In the past decade, research on loneliness has expanded rapidly, spurred in part by the development of reliable paper-and-pencil instruments to assess loneliness (see review by Russell, 1982). Studies in the United States, Europe and Britain (reviewed by Peplau and Perlman, 1982) indicate that loneliness is quite common, with perhaps 20 per cent of adults having felt at least moderately lonely in the past few weeks. Although no social group is immune to loneliness, some people are at greater risk than others. Loneliness is most common among adolescents and young adults, and is less often reported by people in older age groups. Married people report less loneliness than the unmarried. The newly divorced and widowed are at high risk, although this tends to diminish over time. Like other forms of psychological distress, loneliness is more common among lower socioeconomic groups. Possible gender differences in loneliness have not been firmly established.

Several personal characteristics increase the risk of loneliness. These include shyness and introversion, low self-esteem and inadequate social skills. There is some evidence that parental rejection and/or divorce may dispose individuals to loneliness. Features of the social environment can also foster loneliness by limiting opportunities for satisfying social relations.

The immediate cause of loneliness is typically some event that produces a significant deficit in a person's social relations. Common precipitating factors include moving to a new school or community, ending a relationship through death or divorce, or being physically separated from loved ones. Although social transitions such as these can be very distressing, most people appear to cope with them effectively by re-establishing satisfactory social relations. In a minority of cases, however, severe loneliness persists over time and can have disturbing consequences. In adults, chronic loneliness has been linked to depression and suicidal tendencies. In adolescents, loneliness has been associated with school problems, delinquency and running away from home. Therapeutic approaches to helping the severely lonely are currently being developed (Rook and Peplau, 1982; Young, 1982).

Letitia Anne Peplau
University of California, Los Angeles

References

Moustakas, C. E. (1972), *Loneliness and Love*, Englewood Cliffs, N. J.

Peplau, L. A. and Perlman, D. (eds) (1982), *Loneliness: A Sourcebook of Current Theory, Research and Therapy*, New York.

Rook, K. S. and Peplau, L. A. (1982), 'Perspectives on helping the lonely', in L. A. Peplau and D. Perlman (eds), *Loneliness: A Sourcebook of Current Theory, Research and Therapy*, New York.

Rubenstein, C. M. and Shaver, P. (1982), *In Search of Intimacy*, New York.

Russell, D. (1982), 'The measurement of loneliness', in L. A. Peplau and D. Perlman (eds), *Loneliness: A Sourcebook of Current Theory, Research and Therapy*, New York.

Weiss, R. S. (1973), *Loneliness: The Experience of Emotional and Social Isolation*, Cambridge, Mass.

Young, J. (1982), 'Loneliness, depression and cognitive therapy: theory and applications', in L. A. Peplau and D. Perlman (eds), *Loneliness: A Sourcebook of Current Theory, Research and Therapy*, New York.

Mental Health

The categories of mental health and mental illness have to be understood against the backdrop of the social institutions and practices which gave rise to them; and to do this, we need to set the whole in historical context.

Mental illness replaced earlier nineteenth-century concepts of 'madness' or 'insanity'. This was not primarily because of changing beliefs about the cause of mental disturbances, but because the medical profession had gained control of their management. Psychiatry arose hand in hand with the asylum system, but at the outset the latter was conceived as a social remedy for a social problem: if anything, doctors captured this territory *despite* their association with physical theories and treatments, not because of it. Thus, the concepts of mental health and illness were not closely tied to a physical approach to mental disorders. In the nineteenth century, indeed, the most significant feature of mental illness was not its cause but its treatment – incarceration in an asylum. Mental patients at this time were defined as a group primarily by the danger they were seen to pose to themselves or others, a danger which could not be contained in any other way.

The asylum became in practice a last resort when no hope remained for the patient, but in this century the fight against mental illness was taken outside its walls and into the home, work-place and school, where interventions could be made before problems had become intractable. The invention of psychological theories and treatments, in which Freud played a key role, greatly facilitated this spread. Treatment moved from the asylum to the consulting-room, and the meanings of mental illness and mental health shifted accordingly. A new range of illnesses (most importantly, the neuroses) was recognized, and a new range of professions – social work, psychotherapy and the various branches of psychology – arose alongside psychiatry.

Rather than being seen as dangerous, the mental patient was now primarily someone who could not cope with his allotted tasks in life: mental illness was seen as partial and reversible (Armstrong, 1980). Mental health, in the rhetoric of the influential 'mental hygiene movement' founded in America in 1909, became equated with productiveness, social adjustment, and contentment – 'the good life' itself.

The promise of this approach as a panacea for all human ills, coupled with the enormous potential market it opened up to professionals, led to a huge increase in mental health services by the middle of this century. A key factor in the creation of this 'therapeutic state' was the adoption by the mental health professions of a 'scientific' image: in this way, their interventions came to be seen as applications of a value-free, ideologically neutral technology, after the fashion of Comte's 'positivism'.

Social scientists have approached mental health in two main ways. The first is to explore the connection between mental illnesses and aspects of the social environment. Classic studies in this mould are those of Hollingshead and Redlich (1958), who found an increased incidence of mental illness in lower social classes; Brenner (1973), who associated mental illness and economic cycles; and Brown and Harris (1978), who identified predisposing and precipitating factors in women's depression. Though this approach can be seen as merely an extension of the psychiatric enterprise, it nevertheless suggests that to treat environmentally-related conditions as cases of individual malfunctioning may be a form of 'blaming the victim' (Ryan, 1972). In this light, the role of psychiatrists emerges as a fundamentally conservative one: to alleviate the stresses inherent in the social order, while removing any threat to that order itself. It is implicit in the psychiatric concept of 'maladjustment' that it is the individual who has to adapt to society, and not the other way round.

Nevertheless, in the heyday of psychiatric expansionism in the US (the 1950s and early 1960s), some psychiatrists argued that the reform of adverse social conditions was a valid part of psychiatry's mandate after all. Yet financial cutbacks, professional inhibitions, and a political shift to the right soon nipped this 'preventive' psychiatry in the bud.

The second approach adopted by social scientists challenges the very notion of mental illness, and questions the motives that lie behind professional interventions. (Such questioning is invited by the seemingly arbitrary variations in psychiatric nosology, diagnosis and treatment between different times, places and practitioners.) One line of argument focuses on the way in which the field has been shaped by professional self-interest and financial or political factors (for example, profiteering by the drug companies): this critique runs parallel to that made by Illich (1977) and Freidson (1970) of physical medicine. Such an approach has been adopted by historians who have set out to correct the 'triumphalist' picture which professions tend to present of their own history – a picture in which the cumulative victories of reason and humanity culminate inevitably in the achievements of the present.

Other commentators, however, take the argument a step further: they treat mental health as an ideological concept, concealing highly problematic notions about how people should live, and regard the professions that deal with it as agencies of social control. This critique came to the fore in the 1960s, via the work of Foucault (1961), Szasz (1961), Goffman (1961), Scheff (1966) and 'anti-psychiatrists' such as Laing (1960). These writers were not simply claiming that the labelling of certain conditions as 'pathological' was value-laden and culture-bound, for, as Sedgwick (1982) pointed out, the same is true of physical conditions. The critique of psychiatry went further, in claiming that the so-called 'symptoms' were in fact meaningful and freely-chosen acts.

This criticism seems warranted when psychiatry stops people from doing what they want, by means of physical or chemical intervention – for example, political dissidents in the Soviet Union, homosexuals in the West, or (according to Shrag and Divoky, 1975) the million or so American schoolchildren kept under permanent sedation to prevent 'hyperactivity'. Such an analysis seems inapplicable, however, when treatment is actively sought by people anxious to get rid of their 'symptoms'. Moreover, some treatments (especially psychotherapy) claim to increase autonomy, not to diminish it. To treat mental illness as deviance pure and simple is to ignore essential distinctions between 'mad' and 'bad' behaviour – chiefly, the fact that the former is regarded as not making sense, and not under the control of the individual. A straightforward social control model of the mental health professions is therefore limited in its applications.

This is not to say, however, that the remaining instances lack any political significance and are purely therapeutic in character. Behind the concept of mental health lie numerous presuppositions about norms of work, education and family life; and the mental health professions are probably instrumental in maintaining these norms, by influencing not just problem cases but our way of making sense of the world. (Feminists, for example, have argued that psychiatry powerfully reinforces women's traditional role in society (Chessler, 1972).) But if this is a social control mechanism, it is one which has been largely internalized by the population itself. Foucault (1980) goes further, arguing that the power of this mechanism is not 'repressive' but 'productive', since it actually *creates* forms of subjectivity and social life.

Plenty of instances still remain of repression in the name of mental health – as the activities of civil rights organizations and patients' groups testify – and the most convincing analysis is perhaps that of Castel *et al.* (1982), who see the 'hard' and 'soft' methods of treatment as an ensemble, each depending on the other to be fully effective. Although this idea has obvious validity, it is doubtful whether an adequate understanding of the place of mental health in modern society will ever be achieved by trying to impose the same model on such diverse phenomena as lobotomy, forcible incarceration, marital counselling, psychoanalysis and encounter groups.

David Ingleby
University of Utrecht

References

Armstrong, D. (1980), 'Madness and coping', *Sociology of Health and Illness*, 2.

Brenner, H. (1973), *Mental Illness and the Economy*, Cambridge, Mass.

Brown, G. and Harris, T. (1978), *Social Origins of Depression*, London.

Castel, F., Castel, R. and Lovell, A. (1982), *The Psychiatric Society*, New York.

Chessler, P. (1972), *Women and Madness*, New York.

Foucault, M. (1971), *Madness and Civilization*, New York. (Original French, *Histoire de la folie*, Paris, 1961.)

Foucault, M. (1980), 'Truth and power', in *Power/Knowledge: Selected Interviews and Other Writings 1972–1977*, Hassocks.

Freidson, E. (1970), *Professional Dominance*, New York.

Goffman, E. (1961), *Asylums: Essays on the Social Situation of Mental Patients and Other Inmates*, New York.

Hollingshead, A. B. and Redlich, F. C. (1958), *Social Class and Mental Illness*, New York.

Illich, I. (1977), *Disabling Professions*, London.

Laing, R. D. (1960), *The Divided Self*, London.

Ryan, W. (1972), *Blaming the Victim*, New York.

Scheff, T. (1966), *Being Mentally Ill: A Sociological Theory*, London.

Sedgwick, P. (1982), *Psycho Politics*, London.

Shrag, P. and Divoky, D. (1975), *The Myth of the Hyperactive Child and Other Means of Child Control*, New York.

Szasz, T. (1961), *The Myth of Mental Illness*, New York.

Further Reading

Ingleby, D. (ed.) (1980), *Critical Psychiatry: The Politics of Mental Health*, New York.

Penology

Penology is the study of penalties (from the Greek ποινή: penalty), although in its broadest sense it is also concerned with the consequences and merits of attempting to deal with various kinds of conduct by criminal prohibition ('criminalizing'). It includes the study of penal codes of law, but also investigation of the ways in which such penal codes are applied by courts in practice, and the manner in which each type of penal measure is applied. For example, even when a penal code appears to oblige courts to pronounce a sentence (such as imprisonment for 'life' in the case of murder), there are ways of avoiding this (such as convicting the offender of a less serious charge of homicide); and most penal systems provide legal devices by which a sentence of imprisonment can be terminated before its nominal end. Penologists are interested in all such expedients, and in the criteria which are used by courts, administrators and other personnel to make distinctions between offenders, whether for such purposes or for other reasons. Other reasons may include the belief that certain types of offender are more likely than others to respond to certain regimes, or on the other hand that some prisoners are so 'dangerous' that they must be given special sentences, detained longer than is normal for the offence, or given freedom only under specially strict conditions.

An important task of penologists is to provide answers to the question 'How effective is this (or that) measure?' Effectiveness is usually assessed by reconvictions or rearrests, although this is not without problems. For example it cannot take account of offences of which the offender is not suspected; the follow-up period must be substantial; in some jurisdictions rearrests or reconvictions for minor offences are not recorded centrally. The most serious problem, however, is the difficulty of being sure that offenders who remain free of rearrests during the follow-up period would not have remained free if otherwise dealt with: for example, if merely discharged without penalty. In consequence, follow-up studies must usually be content with *comparing* the reconviction rates after different measures. Even so, they have to take into account the fact that courts are selective, and do not allocate offenders randomly to different measures (a few 'random allocation studies' have been achieved, but only for rather specific groups of offenders or offences: see Farrington, 1983). The criteria used to allot offenders to different measures may themselves be associated with higher or lower reconviction rates. For instance, the more previous convictions in a man's record, the more likely he is to be reconvicted, quite apart from any effect which a sentence may have on him. Again, offenders whose offences usually involve theft, burglary, drunkenness or exhibitionism are more likely to be reconvicted than those who commit serious sexual offences or personal violence. Statistical devices have to be used to allow for this, for example, by subdividing samples into 'high-' 'medium- ' and 'low-risk groups'. It is often said that when such precautions are taken the differences between reconviction rates following such different measures as imprisonment, fines and probation tend to disappear, and that the choice of sentence therefore makes no difference to a person's likelihood of reconviction, or not enough difference to justify expensive measures: but this is probably an oversimplification (as was eventually conceded by the chief exponent of the 'nothing works school' in the 1970s, Martinson, 1974, 1979).

In any case, other possible aims of penal measures have to be taken into account. Psychiatrists, for example, usually regard themselves as primarily concerned with the mental health of those committed to their charge by criminal courts; and social workers – including many probation officers – regard their clients' financial and family problems as more important than their legal transgressions.

Whether these views are accepted or not, some penal measures are valued as general deterrents, in the belief that even if they do not often affect the conduct of those who have experienced them, they discourage potential offenders who have not yet committed offences (Beyleveld, 1980). The efficacy of general deterrents has been exaggerated, for example by the supporters of capital punishment: statistical comparisons of jurisdictions which have abolished or retained the death penalty, or of decades in the same jurisdiction preceding and following abolition, suggest that the substitution of long periods of imprisonment for the death penalty does not affect rates of intentional homicide. In plain terms, potential murderers who think before they kill are as likely to be deterred by 'life' as by death. Whatever the penalty, however, its deterrent efficacy depends to a great extent on people's own estimates of the probability of being detected and punished. For some people this seems immaterial; but they tend to be those who commit impulsive or compulsive crimes.

Another aim of some penal measures is simply to protect other people against a repetition of the offence by the offender concerned, usually by some degree of incapacitation. Incapacitation may take the form of long detention, disqualification from certian activities (such as driving or engaging in certain occupations), or surgery (for example, castration for rapists). The more severe types of incapacitating measure are controversial, the chief objection being that the probability of the offender's repeating his offence seldom approaches certainty, and is often less than 50:50 (Floud and Young, 1981).

This illustrates a more general tendency in recent years to

acknowledge the relevance of jurisprudence for penology. Scepticism about the efficacy of corrective or deterrent measures, together with the excessive use of very long detention in the name of therapeutic treatment, has revived the classical emphasis on the need for penalties to reflect the culpability of the offender. The underlying Kantian morality of this was never quite abandoned by jurists in West Germany; but the revival of it in the US and Scandinavia is an important phenomenon, although lacking the sophistication of German jurists (Von Hirsch, 1976).

English judges – and, quite independently, Durkheimian sociologists – have contributed yet another notion. Without necessarily accepting the retributive view (which has both difficulties and dangers), they hold that penalties have an important 'expressive' or 'symbolic' function, declaring publicly the moral disapproval with which most people regard harmful offences (Walker, 1978). Some English judges have even stated that an important task of sentencers is to lead public opinion, although this seems to exaggerate the attention and respect which the public pay to sentences (Walker and Marsh, 1984). More tenable is the proposition that sentences *reflect* people's disapproval: the question is whether sentencers are selected or trained so as to be sure of reflecting the views of the law-abiding public, particularly in societies with heterogeneous moralities.

Other subjects in which penologists have interested themselves are the rights of offenders, especially those recognized by conventions (such as those of the United Nations or European Economic Community); the protection of offenders against avoidable stigma; and the rights of victims to compensation,- whether from the State or the offender, and to other forms of care.

Nigel Walker
University of Cambridge

References
Beyleveld, D. (1980), *A Bibliography on General Deterrence Research*, Westmead.

Farrington, D. P. F. (1983), 'Randomised experiments on crime and justice', in M. Tonry and N. Morris (eds), *Crime and Justice*, Vol. IV, Chicago.

Floud, J. and Young, W. (1981), *Dangerousness and Criminal Justice*, London.

Martinson, T. (1974), 'What works?', *Public Interest*, 35.

Martinson, T. (1979), 'New findings, new views', *Hofstra Law Review*, 7.

Von Hirsch, A. (1976), *Doing Justice, the Choice of Punishments: Report of the Committee for the Study of Incarceration*, New York.

Walker, N. (1978), 'The ultimate justification', in C. F. H. Tapper (ed.), *Crime, Proof and Punishment: Essays in Memory of Sir Rupert Cross*, London.

Walker, N. and Marsh, C. (1984), 'Do sentences affect public disapproval?', *British Journal of Criminology*.

See also: *capital punishment; criminology; punishment.*

Police

To police is to control some people in the interests of more powerful people. In a sense police are 'the state made flesh'. They are unique in being armed, uniformed, legal representatives of government and the judiciary, visibly present in society and empowered to interfere directly in citizens' daily lives. The police organization is closely associated with crime; yet much police work is not related to crime, while many other agencies also investigate and sanction crimes (such as customs, tax, postal, military, and other regulatory authorities).

In small, homogeneous societies the police function of controlling deviance tends to be adopted by the entire community, whereas in more differentiated societies specific officials are appointed to maintain order. In England there exists a line of functionaries, first formalized in the offices of 'constable' and 'sheriff' under the Normans, who performed a policing role but then largely in a manner that was voluntary, local, and restricted in powers. The formation of nation states in Europe witnessed the development of recognizable police organizations employed to control and manipulate politics and the opponents of the state. Napoleon imposed a dual model in Western-European countries comprising a centralized semi-military force, primarily for public order, and local forces for the general police function. In contrast, the formation of the 'new police', with the founding of the Metropolitan Police in London in 1829, ushered in an alternative style: based on local units and ostensibly local control (with policemen not carrying firearms and answerable to the courts, *not* the state), it shaped a model for Britain, its colonies, and the United States. But there still exists enormous variety across cultures in terms of police structure, powers and performance.

Police in Western societies generally concern themselves with maintaining public order, preventing crime, regulating traffic, performing a range of services, collecting political intelligence, and apprehending (and sometimes also prosecuting) criminals. Theories on the police differ widely: a Marxist would see them as pawns of ruling-class hegemony aimed at oppressing the working class, whereas a functionalist might emphasize the integrative role they play in promoting social solidarity. This diversity can partly be explained by the ideological content of policing, which is intimately related to the legal control of the state and to moral values (as in enforcement related to vice, gambling, and alcohol), and about which opinions vary radically, and partly by the dubious reputation of specific agencies (for example, the Gestapo, KGB, CIA, South African Police), in terms of conducting political repression. These negative associations are reinforced by the fact that police form something of a problem profession and have frequently been accused of brutality, corruption, racial prejudice and abuse of citizens's rights. A perennial debate surrounding police relates to restrictions on their power and their ability to undermine effective control of their conduct (Punch, 1983): in short, who controls the controllers?

Research on the police commenced some thirty years ago, and has not led to a coherent subfield within the social sciences (Manning, 1977). Most projects are confined to low-level, urban policing in a few Western countries, but the results fairly consistently reveal that policemen rarely use violence; rarely deal with crime (that is, patrol officers); focus predominantly on 'petty', visible, street-crime (and infrequently on élite or 'white-collar' crime); engage in a wide range of welfare functions; employ wide discretion in enforcement, and that enforcement has little impact on patterns of crime. Various sources also indicate that police work can support practices where laws are systematically bent or broken, where prisoners are abused and denied their rights, where perks and venality are institutionalized, and where judicial guidelines are undermined (Rubinstein, 1973). Two influences have promised improvements in some traditional defects of policing: external pressure has sponsored norms of accountability and responsibility, while fiscal and manpower constraints have imposed more efficient managerial styles. There remains a degree of friction between prescriptions for the police as either a decentralized, broad, social agency responsive to the immediate community, or as a sophisticated, professional, technologically equipped instrument for tackling serious crime (some departments manage to unite both in a pattern of antagonistic co-operation).

Imagery and debate on the police is polarized and contradictory: they are the thin-blue line protecting society from a wave of rapacious criminality, or else they are a bunch of prejudiced, head-cracking sadists. An understanding of the world of the police reveals that it itself is ambivalent, and we should remain alive to the differences *between* policemen and not exaggerate the extent to which agencies are monolithic and views within them unanimous. Police work is imbued with moral symbolism and laudable aims, but the dilemmas of the work can promote a culture that is bawdy, blasphemous, and hedonistic and a style that is posited on lies, falsification, deception, and manipulation of evidence, suspects and informants. The police are forced to engage in 'dirty work' and they can become 'schizophrenic', flitting between good and evil, the commendable and the reprehensible. Policemen have to cope with the discrepancy between legally defined work presented to outsiders and the messy confused reality of working the street.

At the macro level there is no doubt that the police form a crucial, powerful, and potentially sinister element of control within the state apparatus. At the micro level, however, work may be characterized by boredom, sloth, frustration, horseplay and two-finger typing. Discrepant expectations and the nature of the work (witnessing violence and suffering, and, for the detective, the potentially polluting and seductive web of under-world connections) can lead to feelings of bitterness and be-trayal, with the danger of occupational paranoia where police-men feel isolated and aggrieved. At both levels, macro and micro, the police are potentially dangerous and clearly need to be subject to constant vigilance, while their reputation and performance are significant indicators of the moral health of a society (Goldstein, 1977). Perhaps everyone concerned with the police should strive to undermine the fatalistic notion that society gets the police it deserves.

Maurice Punch
Nijenrode, The Netherlands School of Business

References
Goldstein, H. (1977), *Policing a Free Society*, Cambridge, Mass.
Manning, P. K. (1977), *Police Work*, Cambridge, Mass.
Punch, M. (ed.) (1983), *Control in the Police Organization*, Cambridge, Mass.
Rubinstein, J. (1973), *City Police*, New York.
See also: *crime and delinquency; criminology; penology.*

Pornography

A succession of 'moral panics' has dictated the form and focus of much pornographic research. The pattern has typically been one of violent dispute between those for whom pornography constitutes a fundamental threat and those who seek to combat censorship and repressive legislation in the name of rights and freedoms of expression. Social science played a central role in such arguments – which dominated the scene until the late 1970s – yet, paradoxically, without having any real effects on public debate or legislative action.

The traditional combatants in the pornography debate may be loosely grouped into 'moral' and 'liberal' camps. The moral camp take the initiative, proposing both a general and a specific argument. Most broadly they claim that pornography is damaging to the moral fabric of society, undermining family life, basic values, and the quality of our culture. Social scientists have remained conspicuously silent on most of such general issues, other than to observe occasionally that what is 'moral decline' from one point of view may look like acceptable social change from another. Modern society, after all, is hardly characterized by a consensus on matters moral. But social science has had more to say about the moral camp's more specific claims. The typical argument here is that evidence shows the following: that rising trends in the statistics of violent and/or sexual crimes are associated with a 'rising tide of pornography'; and that specific individuals are demonstrably harmed, directly or indirectly, by the consumption of pornography. However, in support of such claims, the moral compaigners make highly selective use of social-science research – the British NVLA, for example, refer constantly to the work of John Court, while ignoring criticisms of it and alternative research findings.

The essentially defensive response of the liberal camp has been to emphasize the massive inconsistency of research findings in the 'effects' area, and to underline the well-known difficulties of developing a coherent causal interpretation of trend statistics. At the heart of their case lies the claim that unless harmful consequences be clearly demonstrated, there is no justification for curtailing an adult individual's freedom to consume privately whatever cultural materials he wishes. This is most lucidly expressed in the Williams Committee report on *Obscenity and Film Censorship*, the most refined example of the liberal position. The committee rejects both the widely publicized claims of the moral camp, as well as the less familiar case that defends pornography because of its alleged beneficial or cathartic effects: in both cases, they conclude, the evidence is insufficient.

One important consequence of public debate having taken this particular form has been an overwhelming focus of research attention in the area of *individual* effects and harms. This has made it difficult to introduce less individualistic alternative conceptualizations of the effects of pornography. In recent years, however, some feminist writers and researchers have sought to shift the terms of the debate. While conceding that it may not be possible to demonstrate satisfactorily the harmful effects on individuals, they argue that the damaging consequences of pornography are real enough. Inasmuch as pornographic materials articulate and express demeaning, antagonistic, and violent attitudes to women, they serve both to diffuse beliefs and to legitimate actions which are unjust and practically damaging to the interests of women. At its clearest, this way of approaching the question extends the concept of 'effects' into a more macroscopic cultural domain in which it is the legitimation and diffusion of sexism which is at issue. Interestingly, this has the consequence of restricting the notoriously vague term pornography to those cultural materials that express particular kinds of views about women; offensiveness, obscenity, and eroticism cease to be central questions. Though this conceptual transition is as yet incomplete, and much of the current literature confusing,• there is now some reason to hope for research that will transcend the restrictive terms imposed by past public debate.

Andrew Tudor
University of York, England

Further Reading
Cline, V. B. (1970), *Where Do We Draw the Line?*, Provo, Utah.
Wilson, W. and Goldstein, M. (eds) (1973), 'Pornography: attitudes, use and effects', *Journal of Social Issues*, 29.

Poverty

The notion of poverty and the reality of attitudes and behaviour towards those classed as poor occur and recur in many societies and at different historical periods. It is correspondingly easy to assume both homogeneity and continuity in idea and response. It is as if the poor, deserving or undeserving (to use a distinction which, despite the Webbs, dates at least from medieval times), are always with us, and it is the same poor and the same desert or blame to which we refer. Such a tendency is reinforced by the close connection between poverty, a particular response to it (that is, the Poor Laws), and the emergence of the comparatively new discipline of social administration. However, it is essential to recognize that the idea of poverty, responses to the poor and the causes of the condition of poverty vary between societies and over time. In the Apostolic age of the Christian Church, for instance, the poor were extolled as 'the temple of God', but in the early eighteenth century, the dramatist Farquhar could write 'Tis still my maxim, that there's no scandal like rags, nor any crime as shameful as poverty' (*The Beaux Stratagem*).

The ways in which poverty has been more recently conceptualized have undergone striking changes. The 1834 Report of the Royal Commission on the Poor Laws described a long-established use when it distinguished indigence from poverty. The former was 'the state of a person unable to labour, or unable to obtain, in return for his labour, the means of subsistence', whereas poverty referred to the more general condition of 'one who, in order to obtain a mere subsistence, is forced to have recourse to labour'. The idea of mere or simple subsistence held sway throughout the nineteenth century but it came to be questioned largely as a result of attempts at the systematic measurement of poverty in order that some estimate might be formed of the proportion of the society that could be described as poor. The most important study was Charles Booth's *Life and Labour of the People in London*, but it is perhaps Seebohm Rowntree's discussion of primary subsistence poverty that most clearly demonstrated its artificial and asocial basis. 'A family living upon the scale allowed for in this estimate must never spend a penny on railway fare or omnibus . . . . They must never purchase a halfpenny newspaper . . . . They must write no letters to absent children. They must never contribute anything to their church or chapel, or give any help to a neighbour which costs them money' (*A Study of Town Life*, 1899).

Such criticism of subsistence poverty has been extended in the present century. Poverty has come to be seen as a deficiency in resources that significantly hampers or prevents participation in events and relationships that give life meaning. More recently, the idea of poverty has been closely allied with that of inequality. Townsend (1979), carrying on the tradition of measurement, attempts through the idea of relative deprivation to establish both a new and a more objective notion of poverty. In addition, he has successfully argued that poverty should now be seen and measured in a worldwide context.

Changes in conception and an increasing sophistication in measurement should be viewed within the context of the changing social significance of poverty. At different times in Western society the poor have been described and treated as making a special claim on philanthropy or as a burden to be carried by public authority, local or central (so definitions of poverty will encompass those conditions that justify the particular response of state relief). At other times the poor are treated as an affront to social justice or, particularly if they can be additionally described as 'dangerous', 'perishing' or 'undeserving', as a symbolic or actual threat to the social order.

Measures specifically adopted in response to indigence and poverty have played a significant role in maintaining social attitudes to poverty, and they reveal in their working and innovation different beliefs concerning the causes of poverty. So, emphasis has moved from belief that poverty is a consequence of individual fate or fault to the idea that it is a major feature of a shared lower-class culture, or that it results from faulty socialization that is transmitted through the generations. These and other notions of causation struggle with the more simple belief that all that is wrong with the poor is that they do not have enough money.

Historically, the Poor Laws mark the first state intervention and they merit special attention, not simply because their history stretches from medieval times, but also because the English experiences of their operation led directly to the creation of the National Health Service and indirectly to the construction of other social services precisely as an alternative to the Poor Laws. Study of the Poor Laws has undergone noticeable shifts from the massive administrative work of the Webbs, through attempts to link the service more closely to the economic and social conditions of the time, to the recent study of Royal Commission Reports as case-studies in the construction of social reality (Green, 1983). The most important recent systematic attempt to combat poverty was the American War on Poverty launched by President Johnson. This proceeded largely on the assumption that previous attempts had failed to tackle major problems concerning service access, service delivery and service governance.

Noel Timms
University of Leicester

References
Green, B. S. (1983), *Knowing the Poor. A Case-Study in Textual Reality Construction*, London.
Townsend, P. (1979), *Poverty in the United Kingdom*, Harmondsworth.

Further Reading
Himmelfarb, G. (1984), *The Idea of Poverty – England in the Early Industrial Age*, London.
See also: *relative deprivation; social welfare policy.*

Prejudice

The word prejudice means pre-judgement, implying that a prejudiced person is someone who has made up his mind about a certain topic before assessing the relevant information. This sense of pre-judgement has formed an important part of the social psychological concept of prejudice. In addition, three other features are associated with prejudiced beliefs: (1) Prejudice typically refers to beliefs about social groups; it can refer also to judgements about individuals, where an individual is evaluated on the basis of being a member of a particular social group. (2) The belief or judgement is essentially an unfavourable one. Whereas it is logically possible to be prejudiced *in favour* of a group, prejudice usually denotes a negative or hostile attitude *against* a group: racist, anti-Semitic and sexist attitudes would all be considered prime examples of prejudice. (3) A prejudiced belief is assumed to be erroneous or liable to lead the believer into error. A prejudice is not based on a realistic assessment of a social group, nor is contact with the group likely to overturn the prejudices. Thus Allport, in his classic discussion of prejudice, wrote 'pre-judgements become prejudices only if they are not reversible when exposed to new knowledge' (1958).

Part of the prejudiced person's error derives from a tendency to think about social groups in terms of stereotypes. In one of the first social psychological investigations of stereotypes, Katz and Braly (1935) found amongst American college students a widespread tendency to ascribe clichéd descriptions to different social groups: thus the stereotype of Blacks included the traits of being 'superstitious' and 'lazy', that of Jews as 'mercenary' and 'grasping', that of Turks as 'cruel' and 'treacherous', and so on. By thinking in such stereotypes, the prejudiced person not only has an unfavourable concept of the groups as a whole but he also exaggerates the percentage of individuals who might happen to possess the stereotyped trait; in the case of extreme prejudice, he will believe that *all* Jews or *all* Blacks possess the unfavourable traits in question.

Early research into prejudice assumed a direct relation between holding prejudiced beliefs and behaving in a discriminatory way to members of the relevant outgroup. For example, the Bogardus Distance Scale asked respondents whether they would entertain having close relations (such as marriage) or less close relations (such as working in the same place) with particular outgroups. It was assumed that the respondent's replies would predict actual behaviour towards members of outgroups. However, research into attitude theory in general has revealed that the views expressed in attitude questionnaires do not necessarily reflect behaviour.

In consequence, it is now recognized that the relations between prejudice and discrimination are more complex than was formerly thought.

Among the many theories used to explain the psychological roots of prejudice, it is possible to distinguish between motivational and learning theories. Motivational theories have sought to relate prejudiced attitudes to personality defects or to unfulfilled yearnings within the individual. These are often called 'scapegoat' theories in that they assume that the victims of prejudice are being irrationally blamed for ills that reside within the prejudiced person. One such scapegoat theory is the frustration–aggression theory (originally proposed by Dollard *et al.* (1939) and reformulated by Berkowitz (1962)). It asserts that prejudice arises when an individual has been angered by some frustration and is unable, for some reason or other, to direct this anger back on to the source of the frustration. Instead, the anger is displaced onto an innocent target. This theory has been employed, for instance, to explain why minority groups may become targets of increased prejudice in times of economic deprivation. Another motivational theory is that of Adorno *et al.* (1950) which seeks to account for prejudice in terms of the repressed hostility of authoritarian-type personalities: such people, it is argued, direct their hostilities on to weak outgroups because of their own personal inadequacies.

Motivational theories as general theories of prejudice are limited. For example, they fail to explain why particular targets are chosen for prejudice and not others; they also tend to understate the extent to which prejudiced beliefs might be the product of learning. Pettigrew's comparison of the different levels of prejudice in South Africa and the United States showed that personality factors were less important than the existence of cultural traditions (Pettigrew, 1958). In the case of White South Africans these traditions had resulted in prejudiced beliefs, which were so widely accepted that they had become normative and, by contrast, tolerance was regarded as socially deviant. Thus, within such a prejudiced society, children are likely to be socialized through learning into acquiring prejudiced beliefs; the displacement of underlying motivations need not feature in the process.

Much of the recent research in social psychology has concentrated upon the cognitive aspects of prejudice and investigates prejudice in terms of the ways people generally perceive and make sense of the world. This research suggests that a large degree of prejudiced thinking is not the result of 'abnormal' psychological processes. Jerome Bruner (1958) and Henri Tajfel

(1981) have indicated that people are not passive recipients of information; rather, they try to make sense of incoming stimuli. Thus 'normal' perception involves a certain amount of error and simplification as information is categorized and assessed according to pre-judgements, which in turn determine what is perceived or experienced. Stereotyped thinking represents an extreme case of such processes, with the stereotype influencing what aspects of the social world are selected for attention and how these aspects are interpreted. For example, a person who views a particular group as lazy will often unconsciously seek confirmation of his stereotype and ignore contradictory evidence. In addition, ambiguous evidence will be interpreted in support of the idea that the group is lazy, and the result will be a perception of that group with a systematic distortion which appears to confirm the stereotype. If the stereotype is widely held within a society, then not only will it pass as common sense, and social pressures will promote the stereotype, but cognitive processes may prevent believers from becoming aware of their own biases.

Michael Billig
Loughborough University

References

Adorno, T. W., Frenkel-Brunswik, E., Levinson, D. J. and Sanford, R. N. (1950), *The Authoritarian Personality*, New York.

Allport, G. W. (1958), *The Nature of Prejudice*, Garden City, N.Y.

Berkowitz, L. (1962), *Aggression: A Social Psychological Analysis*, New York.

Bruner, J. S. (1958), 'Social psychology and perception', in E. E. Maccoby, T. W. Newcomb and E. L. Hartley (eds), *Readings in Social Psychology*, London.

Dollard, J. L., Doob, W., Miller, N. E., Mowrer, O. H. and Sears, R. R. (1939), *Frustration and Aggression*, New Haven.

Katz, D. and Braly, K. W. (1935), 'Racial prejudice and racial stereotypes', *Journal of Abnormal and Social Psychology*, 30.

Pettigrew, T. F. (1958), 'Personality and sociocultural factors in intergroup attitudes: a cross national comparison', *Journal of Conflict Resolution*, 2.

Tajfel, H. (1981), *Human Groups and Social Categories*, Cambridge,

Further Reading

Hamilton, D. L. (1979), 'A cognitive-attributional analysis of stereotyping', in L. Berkowitz (ed.), *Advances in Experimental Social Psychology*.

See also: *conflict resolution; ethnic relations; labelling theory.*

Prostitution

Prostitution is the sale and purchase of sexual relations. While universal, its prevalence, the specific forms it takes, and how it is morally evaluated and legally dealt with, can all vary greatly. There can be homosexual prostitutes (of either sex), as well as male prostitutes who sell sexual favours to women. But it is the sale of female sexuality to men that has usually been the predominant pattern, and (at times) has given rise to the greatest social concern.

Owing, perhaps, to the influence of psychological and social-service orientations, the 'causes' of prostitution often are addressed through the study of individual prostitutes. This misleading view of prostitution, as being something 'done by' prostitutes – whilst ignoring the causal significance of male demand for their services – is itself indicative of the sexual double standard on which the phenomemon of prostitution rests. Numerous analysts have noted the hypocrisy that this standard entails, and have also drawn an analogy between the commercial sale of sex and the common exchange within marriage of sexual favours for financial security and social standing (for example, Engels, 1942 [1891]). Both patterns reflect the tendency, found to some extent in most societies, for the dominant males to treat women as their 'sexual property' (Lévi-Strauss, 1969 [1949]).

Recent feminist analyses emphasize the oppressiveness of a system that socially and legally punishes individual prostitutes, while at the same time breeding male demand for prostitution, limiting women's other means of attaining a livelihood, and encouraging girls and women generally to view their sexuality as a commodity to be 'capitalized' on in order to enhance their life chances. From this standpoint (James *et al.*, 1975), there is no mystery regarding either the 'causes' of the individual prostitute's job choice or the prevalence of prostitution as a general social pattern. Wishing to express their solidarity with prostitute women, yet at the same time frequently considering prostitution overall to be an exploitative by-product of sexual inequality and sexist value distortions, feminists have confronted something of a dilemma in assessing public-policy measures and proposals. Historical studies have shown, furthermore, that anti-prostitution campaigns (Walkowitz 1980; Rosen 1982) often display or evoke general tendencies towards sexual repression and paternalistic control.

Laws against prostitution are usually ineffective in curbing the practice. Their administration typically involves routine harassment and minor punishment of prostitutes (while largely ignoring their customers) and efforts to restrict blatant public solicitation. Contemporary feminists assert that such laws oppress prostitute women. They tend, however, to oppose the 'legalization' or regulation of prostitution – on the ground that this confers on the practice a governmental stamp of legitimacy. An alternative policy of 'decriminalization' (eliminating laws that victimize the prostitute, but not involving the state in the regulation of prostitution) is often preferred as a short-term ameliorative. Nevertheless, most feminists also advocate the eventual elimination (or substantial reduction) of prostitution. To that end, they urge ongoing efforts to reduce the institutionalized sexism in which they believe prostitution to be largely grounded.

Edwin M. Schur
New York University

References
Engels, F. (1942 [1891]), *The Origin of the Family, Private Property, and the State*, 4th edn, New York.
James, J. *et al.* (1975), *The Politics of Prostitution*, Seattle.
Lévi-Strauss, C. (1969 [1949]), *The Elementary Structures of Kinship*, Boston. (Original French, *Les Structures élémentaires de la parenté*, Paris.)
Rosen, R. (1982), *The Lost Sisterhood*, Baltimore.
Walkowitz, J. (1980), *Prostitution and Victorian Society*, Cambridge.

Further Reading
Beauvoir, S. de (1953), *The Second Sex*, New York.
See also: *pornography; sexual behaviour*.

Public Health

The Dictionary of Epidemiology (Last, 1983) defines public health as 'one of the efforts organized by society to protect, promote and restore the people's health. It is the combination of sciences, skills, and beliefs that are directed to the maintenance and improvement of the health of all the people through collective or social actions. The programmes, services and institutions involved emphasize the prevention of disease and the health needs of the population as a whole. Public health activities change with changing technology and social values, but the goals remain the same: to reduce the amount of disease, premature death, and disease-produced discomfort and disability in the population. Public health is thus a social institution, a discipline, and a practice.'

The practice of public health is to a large extent a political activity, and its approach is coloured by the degree to which health care is a private or public matter in the community. Approaches can range from, on the one hand, the 'rats, lice and sewers' circumscription of public health which occurs where individual health care is seen as a primarily time-limited contract between (potential) healer and (potential) healee, to the broad encompassment of all the problems which may affect the health of a population (that is, practically everything), on the other. The latter approach is not new and was recognized by Winslow in 1951: 'No sound distinction . . . can be drawn between "sanitation", "preventive medicine", "curative medicine", "health medicine", "health promotion", and "improvement of standards of living". All are part of a comprehensive public-health programme in the modern sense.' The declaration of Alma-Ata (1978), endorsed by the Member States of WHO, goes even further: 'Economic and social development . . . is of basic importance to the fullest attainment of health for all. . . . The promotion and protection of the health of the people . . . contributes to a better quality of life and to world peace.'

Public health therefore is an area where traditional practitioners of medicine and healing represent only a fraction of the troupe of actors: mathematicians, engineers, sociologists, managers, educators, political scientists, theologians and others have all played a role in its development. The latest edition of *Maxcy-Rosenau's Textbook of Public Health and Preventive Medicine* (Last, 1980) stresses the degree to which 'the range and scope of the science and skills required for the practice of public health have extended since 1913', when the first edition of *Rosenau's Preventive Medicine and Hygiene* was published (note the change of title, which last occurred in the 1956 edition). This constitutes a welcome extension in scope. It must, however, be borne in mind that the main tools which support the effectiveness of public health – that is, enable it to affect favourably the health of a community – include (1) fundamental and applied research in epidemiology in order to identify and quantify the problems of the community and to measure the impact of interventions, and (2) political decision-taking, which assists in the implementation of solutions to these problems. Physicians and other members of the health professions should be no worse than average at politics and, by virtue of their training, they are usually well prepared to take decisions. Even in the face of calls for demedicalization of the practice of medicine (see Illich, 1975), one might thus wish to retain a major role for epidemiol-

ogically-minded physicians and health professionals in the practice of public health.

M. C. Thuriaux
World Health Organization
Regional Office for Europe, Copenhagen

References
Illich, I. (1975), *Medical Nemesis. The Expropriation of Health*,
New York.
Last, J. (ed.) (1980), *Maxcy-Rosenau's Textbook of Public Health
and Preventive Medicine*, 11th edn, New York.
Last, J. (ed.) (1983), *Dictionary of Epidemiology*, New York.
Winslow, C. E. A. (1951), *The Cost of Sickness and the Price of
Health*, Geneva.

Punishment

Punishment is an intended evil. At the macro-level, discussion
has centred on the reasons for punishment, its effects, the
acceptable forms of punishment, and the relationships between
social structure and level of punishment. At the micro-level –
which will not be covered here – the discussion has concerned
the effects of punishments as opposed to rewards on the ability
to learn.

There are two main sorts of justification of punishment: (1)
The natural law position argues that we punish because we
punish, or, in some formulations, we punish because it would
be unjust not to do so. God or Nature demand it. Even if we
live seconds before doomsday, the condemned murderer must
be hanged otherwise justice would not have been done. Often
implicit in this model is a sort of equilibrium theory: evil
balances out evil. The tariff, however, may change over time:
an eye for an eye in biblical time becomes two years of imprisonment – or 500 dollars – in our time. (2) The other major position
is utilitarian: punishment has a purpose; we punish because it
is necessary. Punishment is a means to get offenders (individual
prevention) or potential offenders (general prevention) to obey
the law. The magnitude of the pain inflicted is in this case not

proportionate to the crime but to the intended social purposes. Legal philosophers often attempt to reconcile the two major positions, particularly by insisting that no more pain should be inflicted for reasons of utility than is acceptable according to just desert. The equally logical opposite position – that pain should not be inflicted if it serves no purpose – is more seldom expressed. The empirical study of punishment is closely related to these moral issues. If punishment deters, then the utilitarian position is strengthened.

Criminologists have given much thought to the effects of punishment on the offender himself. In general, they have not been able to identify any particular form of punishment that would seem to reduce the probability of relapse: no one measure (apart from death or castration, of course) appears to work better than any other. Some criminologists even claim that the only thing they have found is that punishments are likely to increase the danger of committing further crimes, because all punishments – even if they are called someting else – imply stigma.

As far as the effects of punishment on other people's behaviour is concerned (that is, the general preventive effects), results of research are more complex both to describe and interpret. These effects are evident when we contrast extreme alternatives. Capital punishment for minor and easily detected offences will reduce them, while the absence of any sanction will encourage them – as we see in situations where the police are out of action. More commonly, the choice lies between degrees of punishment, for example, between one or two years imprisonment. In such cases, there are few indications that one punishment is more effective than another. Even death penalties are not demonstrably more effective deterrents than long prison sentences.

Modern societies differ widely with respect to their penal traditions. Table 1 gives the number of prisoners per 100,000 inhabitants in selected countries. (The figures for Eastern Europe are less reliable than those for the West, and most are from the last years of the 1970s. Those for the US and Western Europe are mainly from the 1980s. In all cases, the definition of 'prison' presents problems.) Eastern-bloc countries generally have higher prison figures than Western countries. Where life is harsh and power relatively uncontrolled, a strict penal policy is likely. The personal safety of the citizens seems only slightly affected by the incarceration rate of a nation. Moscow has one form of security – and insecurity. New York has another.

Table 1

Prisoners per 100,000 inhabitants in selected industrialized countries

USSR	660
USA	280–300
Poland	220–300
DDR	222
Bulgaria	150
Czechoslovakia	142
Austria	118
Yugoslavia	101
BDR	100
Finland	99
England	86
Denmark	68
Sweden	49
Norway	44
The Netherlands	23

What are regarded as acceptable forms of punishment clearly also reflect general cultural traditions. Some countries find it acceptable to punish the whole family, others only the culprit. Some take life, some arms, some testicles, while some limit themselves to depriving the offender of time or money. Welfare states, with their emphasis on reducing suffering, face particular problems in deliberately inflicting suffering. A characteristic solution is to disguise this value-conflict by calling punishment 'treatment', 'education' and so on.

Nils Christie
University of Oslo

Further Reading
Andenaes, J. (1974), *Punishment and Deterrence*, Ann Arbor.
Christie, N. (1981), *Limits to Pain*, Oxford.
Hirsch, A. von (1976), *Doing Justice*, Report of the Committee
   for the Study of Incarceration, New York.
Mathiesen, T. (1974), *The Politics of Abolition*, Oxford.
Rawls, J. (1972), *A Theory of Justice*, Oxford.
See also: *capital punishment; penology; rehabilitation.*

Rape

Rape can be defined socially or legally. The social definition
includes sexual activity in which one partner is an unwilling
participant. Legal definitions yield much greater variability,
with victim non-consent, assailant force, and evidence of sexual
intercourse often required in order to satisfy legal statutes.
Historically, the crime has required a female victim and a male
perpetrator. Research on rape has expanded with increased
social awareness and sensitivity to rape primarily as a result of
the women's movement. The research has developed in two
parallel areas: (1) social research on the societal beliefs about
rape and assumptions about responsibility in rape episodes;
and (2) clinical research on the psychological consequences for
victims and the motivation of rapists.

Social Stereotypes
Social stereotypes regarding rape include a view of the woman
as responsible for preventing the rape, and yet, an assumption
that many women secretly desire and would enjoy being raped.
In addition, most people regard rape as a sexually motivated
crime. Although these stereotypes appear to have little or no
basis in reality, they are evident in the attributions people make
about rape episodes. For example, when asked to provide causal
explanations for the occurrence of a rape, people will assign
increasing responsibility for the rape to the female victim, if she
is assumed to be sexually appealing. Thus an attractive woman
is likely to be judged as more responsible for the rape, as is a
woman who has been sexually active or who has been raped
before. The underlying belief seems to be that a woman is

'asking for it' by being sexually active or attractive. Additionally, the woman is more negatively evaluated if she is regarded as not having struggled sufficiently or as not being emotionally upset by the rape. This tendency to see the victim as playing a causal role in the attack could have serious implications for the social adjustment of the rape victim, as well as the legal disposition of rape cases.

Rapist Motivation

No single explanation applies to all rape cases. The current view, however, is that the crime is not primarily sexually motivated, nor is it routinely a manifestation of psychiatric disorder. Many rapists are married or have ongoing relationships at the time of the crime. One-third or more may experience sexual dysfunction during the attack (such as failure to achieve an erection), and many report finding little or no sexual satisfaction in the rape. The attack, particularly that of a woman by a man, is seen as an expression of power or anger. This hostile nature of the crime may contribute to the victim's psychological suffering.

Victim Reactions

The victims of sexual assault suffer psychologically in a variety of ways. Distressing emotions, particularly anger, fear and anxiety, predominate in the days immediately following the attack. Self-recrimination and guilt over being victimized are also frequent. Sexual functioning is likely to be negatively affected, specific fears may develop, and symptoms of depression (difficulty in sleeping, sadness, appetite loss, etc.) may occur. Victims may also have various other responses, including obsessional thoughts, withdrawal, nightmares and psychophysiological disorders. Psychological support and short-term crisis psychotherapy are desirable. For some victims, however, the psychological distress precipitated by the assault may last for years, requiring more extensive psychological intervention.

Arnie Cann and Lawrence G. Calhoun
University of North Carolina, Charlotte

Further Reading

Berger, V. (1977), 'Man's trial, woman's tribulation: rape cases in the courtroom', *Columbia Law Review*, 77.

Burt, M. R. (1980), 'Cultural myths and supports for rape', *Journal of Personality and Social Psychology*, 38.

Cann, A., Calhoun, L. G., Selby, J. W. and King, H. E. (eds) (1981), 'Rape', *Journal of Social Issues*, 37.

Katz, S. and Mazur, M. A. (1979), *Understanding the Rape Victim*, New York.

Rape Avoidance

There are as many myths about how to avoid rape when attacked as about rape itself. The advice that women were given was consistent with the traditional female role; passive (relax and enjoy it); manipulative ('you're so handsome – why don't we go for a drink first?'); humanistic ('I'm Mary and I don't want to do this but I care about you. Tell me your problems'), and acting 'crazy' (drooling, speaking incoherently). Women were also told not to fight back since it would only excite the assailant.

But since 1976, when the Queen's Bench (1976) study was published, a body of research has accumulated demonstrating that active strategies are more likely to deter the assailant. Talking was rarely effective by itself and the use of physical strategies by women sharply increased the possibility of stopping the rape, with little added risk of serious injury. Two of five women in Bart and O'Brien's (1984) study who were severely injured used *no* strategies and *all* the women who used no strategies were raped. Moreover, raped women who fought back were less likely to suffer depression afterwards.

Bart and O'Brien, comparing fifty-one avoiders with forty-three raped women (self-defined), found differences in socialization, demographic and situational variables, and in strategies used during the attack. While raped women were more likely to plead, avoiders yelled, fled or tried to flee, and used physical strategies. There was also more frequent environmental intervention in the latter cases. Additionally, the more types of strategies used, the higher the probability of avoidance. The avoiders generally focused on not being raped, while the raped women focused on not being killed. The researchers' demographic and socialization variables substantially supported the feminist view that traditional socialization socializes women for victimization.

Pauline B. Bart
University of Illinois, Chicago

References
Bart, P. B. and O'Brien, P. (1984), 'How the women stopped their rapes', *Signs*, vol. 10.
Queen's Bench Foundation (1976), *Rape: Prevention and Resistance*, San Francisco.

Further Reading
Bart, P. B. (1981), 'A study of women who both were raped and avoided rape', *Journal of Social Issues*, 37.
Sanders, W. (1974), *Rape and Woman's Identity*, Beverly Hills, California.

Rehabilitation

Rehabilitation of prisoners may carry three distinct meanings: reform of character, reinstatement in society, and mitigating institutionalized behaviour. Apparently respectable citizens may, however, continue unapprehended with offences of a kind for which they were once imprisoned. Such ambiguity mystifies the study of the treatment not only of offenders but also of Skid Row alcoholics, the psychologically disturbed, neglected children and other members of society regarded as needing help.

There are other problems, besides those of definition, in the evaluation of rehabilitation:

(1) Rehabilitative programmes sometimes change what they claim to achieve – or even for whom they achieve it (Regier, 1979) – once their original ambitious aims meet with failure.

(2) Sociologists consider the viewpoint not only of helpers but also of the helped. Helpers may support rehabilitiation in one sense, but offenders, patients or clients may reject it in another. Thus Davies (1974) defines rehabilitation as 'overcoming the effects of incarceration', whereas a probationer says, 'It would be easier to be back inside.'

(3) All organizations involve controlling people – sometimes very tightly. A consideration for human rights implies that rehabilitation should not be reduced to coercion. The 'latent function' of a rehabilitative organization may be more regimented control. Goffman's analysis of 'total institutions', Foucault's critique of their insidious expansion, and a concern for phenomena like the hospitalization as mentally ill of political dissidents or troublesome relatives (Scheff, 1966) all cast doubt on the assumption that 'rehabilitation' must be intrinsically beneficial.

Maurice Glickman
University of Botswana

References
Davies, M. (1974), *Prisoners of Society: Attitudes and After-Care*, London.
Regier, M. (1979), *Social Policy in Action: Perspectives on the Implementation of Alchohol Reforms*, Lexington, Mass.
Scheff, T. (1966), *Being Mentally Ill*, Chicago.

Further Reading
Glickman, M. (1983), *From Crime to Rehabilitation*, Aldershot.
HMSO (1963), *The Organization of After-Care. Report of the Advisory Council on the Treatment of Offenders*, London.
See also: *penology; punishment.*

Relative Deprivation

Deprivation is relative. People experience resentment or discontent about their condition not necessarily when they are deprived in an absolute sense, but when they feel deprived relative to some standard of comparison. These are the essential concepts behind the theory of relative deprivation (RD). Because a wide range of studies on racial riots, student and feminist protest movements reveal that the participants in these events are generally not the most deprived or disadvantaged of their respective groups, the RD explanation appears to be a plausible alternative to an absolute deprivation thesis.

The first use of the term 'relative deprivation' dates from the Second World War. Samuel Stouffer and his colleagues at the Research Division of the Information Branch of the US Army (1949) employed it in *The American Soldier* as an *ad hoc* explanation for the surprising findings that some objectively better-off soldiers actually experienced greater discontent. Since then, social psychologists, sociologists and political scientists have developed a number of models of relative deprivation in order to explain various personal and collective phenomena.

Stated simply, relative deprivation refers to the negative emotion, variously expressed as anger, resentment, or dissatisfaction, which individuals experience when they compare their situation with some standard or reference. The standard might include other persons, other groups or comparisons with oneself in the past.

In examining the various existing models (see Crosby, 1976; Davis, 1959; Gurr, 1970; Runciman, 1966), it becomes readily apparent that all share some features:

(1) The basic premise of all models is that objective and subjective well-being are not isomorphically related. Every model specifies various cognitive and emotional factors which precede feelings of relative deprivation. Most models regard the two precursory conditions for feelings of relative deprivation as: the absence of some possession or right (referred to as X) and the awareness by the person experiencing RD that another person or another group has X. However, the other conditions, such as deserving X, expecting X, personal responsibility for not having X, vary from model to model.

(2) There is an assumed link between experienced relative deprivation and the attitudinal or behavioural conse-

quences at the personal and collective levels. The various consequences of RD (depending on the theory) are stress, low self-evaluation, attempts at self-improvement, and the growth of social movements, collective violence and even revolutions.

The fundamental process of RD has now been firmly established. Current research efforts are directed at understanding some of the persistent puzzles that remain: When is it that the feeling of RD is followed by action? Why is it that more action is sometimes taken when RD is decreased? What are the distinctions, in terms of antecedents and consequences, between personal RD (a type of personal discontent that occurs when an individual compares his own situation to that of others) and collective RD (feelings of social discontent that occur when an individual compares the situation of his group as a whole to that of an outgroup)? Answers to these questions are likely to emphasize even more the need to consider psychological factors in explaining otherwise incomprehensible events.

Lise Dubé-Simard
University of Montreal

References

Crosby, F. (1976), 'A model of egoistical relative deprivation', *Psychological Review*, 83.

Davis, J. A. (1959), 'A formal interpretation of the theory of relative deprivation', *Sociometry*, 22.

Gurr, T. R. (1970), *Why Men Rebel*, Princeton, New Jersey.

Runciman, W. G. (1966), *Relative Deprivation and Social Justice: A Study of Attitudes to Social Inequality in Twentieth-Century England*, Berkeley and Los Angeles.

Stouffer, S. A., Suchman, E. A., De Vinney, L. C., Star, S. A. and Williams, R. M. (1949), *The American Soldier: Adjustment during Army Life*, vol. 1, Princeton, New Jersey.

Sexual Behaviour

Our knowledge about human sexual behaviour has increased greatly and so has the availability of information about it. And, of course, sexual behaviour itself has changed. Although many social scientists argue that we have experienced more than just a change – perhaps a revolution – others would regard this claim as an overstatement.

Sex is defined here as anything connected with genital stimulation, sexual gratification, reproduction, and the behaviour that accompanies such stimulation, gratification and involvement. Kissing, petting, coitus and masturbation, for example, constitute forms of sexual behaviour and are referred to by the term sex and its derivatives, *sexual* and *sexuality*. Sexual behaviour, when discussed within a particular social context such as premarital, marital, or extramarital sexual behaviour, refers to those acts by an individual (either physically acted out or mentally acted out, as in the case of fantasizing) which involve another individual (imagined or real) and which centre around sexual gratification.

Procreation and Recreation

Sexual interaction has at least two distinct functions: (1) procreation, which accounts for only a tiny portion of coital activity in contemporary society, and (2) recreation, which has always accounted for most sexual interaction, although the extent of recreational sex may be different for males and females. That the extent of recreational sex outweighs that of procreational sex is suggested by the lower birth-rates for both wanted and unwanted children since a generation ago, and by the increase in the frequencies of premarital, marital and extramarital sexual behaviour throughout most of the Western world. Certainly today, recreational sex, whether inside or outside of marriage, is the rule rather than the exception.

There is evidence, however, that the increasing incidence and prevalence of sexual behaviour for purposes other than procreation has not been accompanied by an increased awareness of the consequences and ramifications of such behaviour. Research indicates that in the United States, for example, most never-married, sexually experienced teenage women have engaged in coitus without using contraception. Thus, it is easy to understand why illegitimacy rates and the number of abortions performed for unmarried women have both increased dramatically, and why a significant minority of brides are pregnant on their wedding day. It seems clear that as long as we live in societies which frown upon and are largely unsupportive of pregnancy out of wedlock, and young couples themselves do not desire such pregnancies, a thorough discussion of contraception, pregnancy, childbirth, and the consequences of sexual activity is warranted.

Revolution or Evolution?

The limited, but reasonable, evidence found throughout Western societies suggests that human sexual behaviour has undergone the following changes in recent years:

(1) An increase in the number of individuals having premarital coitus, particularly females.

(2) An increase in the number of partners with whom an individual is likely to have premarital sexual relationships.

(3) Individuals are having their first sexual relationships at earlier ages.

(4) A lesser level of commitment is necessary before individuals become involved in sexual relationships.

(5) A greater frequency of marital coitus.

(6) A greater incidence of extramarital coitus, particularly among women.

(7) A higher proportion of abortions are being given to unmarried women; there is also a higher frequency of abortions among unmarried women.

(8) An increase in the illegitimacy rate among unmarried women, particularly teenagers.

(9) Increased utilization of family-planning services and contraceptives by females of all ages.

(10) Widespread adoption of more effective methods of contraception by women of all ages, social-class levels, religions and races.

(11) More open discussion of, and exposure to, sexuality in books, magazines, films and other media.

(12) More liberal acceptance of alternative life-styles and alter-
      native expressions of sexuality, such as homosexuality.
(13) More freedom for females in initiating informal hetero-
      sexual social contacts and sexual relations.
(14) A greater willingness to talk about sex, to tolerate different
      values and attitudes, and to accept sex, even in cases
      where another individual's standards may be different
      from one's own.

If it is true that these changes have occurred in recent years,
then it might seem evident that, by almost any definition, a
sexual revolution has occurred. But this conclusion is potentially misleading for a number of reasons.

Social scientists have usually pointed to premarital intercourse as the key indicator of sexual revolution, even though
this must surely be only a part of it. If we focus, for the moment,
on premarital sexual behaviour in Western societies, we find
evidence that between the 1920s and the 1960s changes were
minimal. In the years that coincided with the post-war baby
boom, economic prosperity, television, industrialization, and
the increasing impact of mass media, people began to talk
and write often about 'the sexual revolution'. Respected social
scientists and others have declared this revolution to be over
and done with a number of times.

In retrospect, it appears that although sexuality was more
frequently and openly discussed during the 1950s and early
1960s there was, in fact, no dramatic increase in sexual behaviour. It now seems as though we were misled by all the talk,
since the data show only a slight change in actual behaviour.

However, when we look at data collected since the mid-
1960s, we begin to see some noticeable, significant, and at times
dramatic changes in the number of individuals engaging in
premarital intercourse. This trend is best documented in the
United States, but there is some evidence of similar trends in
Europe. Indeed, the incidence has increased moderately for
males during the last decade, and dramatically for females. It
can be said that the females are 'catching up' – at least in terms

of the cumulative number of females who have had at least one coital experience before marriage.

Most of the available data on sexual behaviour, however, concern indicators of frequency and incidence. It is likely that the magnitude of social change must be judged not just on the basis of cumulative incidence, but rather on the nature and quality of the relationships being examined. Thus, although it appeared that females were catching up with males in terms of actual incidence, there were still dramatic differences in their reactions to, feelings about, management of, and socialization for sexual relationships.

A revolution *has* occurred if we are referring to the very significant increase in the prevalence of female sexual activity, both inside and outside of marriage. But 'revolution' is perhaps an overstatement if we consider sexual performance, values, and the attitudes that are more deeply rooted in the socialization process.

Graham B. Spanier
Oregon State University

Further Reading

Kinsey, A., Pomeroy, W., Martin, C. and Gebhard, P. (1948), *Sexual Behavior in the Human Male,* Philadelphia.

Kinsey, A., Pomeroy, W., Martin, C. and Gebhard, P. (1953), *Sexual Behavior in the Human Female*, Philadelphia.

Masters, W. and Johnson, V. (1966), *Human Sexual Response*, Boston.

Masters, W. and Johnson, V. (1970), *Human Sexual Inadequacy*, Boston.

Sorenson, R. C. (1973), *Adolescent Sexuality in Contemporary America*, Cleveland.

See also: *homosexuality; incest behaviour; rape.*

Social Indicators

The social indicator 'movement' in the form of a dedicated body of scholars, numerous books, academic articles, national and international meetings, and a journal of social indicators research is of fairly recent origin under this name. It emerged jointly with a revival of interest in measurement of social change, social analysis and social policy in two places: in the international organizations in the early 1950s and in the United States in the mid-1960s.

Work in the United Nations and other international agencies centred upon measurement of levels of living, particularly in the developing countries. The purpose was to assess need as well as record progress in meeting need. One of the issues at the time was the extent to which concepts and methods of measurement in developed countries were applicable also to developing countries. In the United States, interest in social indicators and related concepts, such as 'social reporting' or 'national goals accounting', arose from academic curiosity and political concern about social trends, the need to consider social change as a totality, and the awareness that there was nothing on the social side corresponding to the well-established economic accounts or economic reports. There was also thought to be an immediate practical application, in the evaluation of programme benefits. Some of these hopes, for instance, to obtain social accounts to match economic accounts, have not been fulfilled for reasons that are now well known: the considerable heterogeneity of 'social' items, absence of a comprehensive social model, lack of a common unit of measurement such as the dollar or pound in economic accounting. Since these early endeavours, use of the term has spread to the majority of developed and to some of the statistically more advanced developing countries. The United Kingdom began its periodical *Social Trends* in 1970; other national reports include *Données Sociales* (France), *Social Indicators* (Trinidad and Tobago), *Life and its Quality in Japan*, *Perspective Canada*.

The Meaning of Indicators

To make a scientific contribution, the term 'social indicators' must be defined so as to distinguish it from other, similar terms as regards both 'indicator' and 'social'. There is so far no agreed definition. Of the several in vogue only the following two-step procedure appears to give a distinct meaning which at the same time is sufficiently broad to provide for a programme of work. A first step is to define the 'fields' of conceptual items which are to be measured. These may be broad, such as 'development' or the 'quality of life of the people in Britain'; or they may be narrow, such as the 'educational status' of a specific local population or the 'health conditions of the Palestinian refugees'. They may be conventional social sectors, such as health or education, or 'domains' as used in French planning to denote problem groups or areas, of which inequality or social problems associated with the process of ageing are examples. Because few such fields or domains can be measured directly, recourse is had to 'indicators'. The second step therefore consists of selecting indicators that are conceptually related to the field, and that, using as few indicators as possible, cover it as comprehensively and precisely as possible. Thus, the health of a refugee population can be described in terms of several discrete components of which the overall level of health services, access to services, health status are examples. None of these can be fully measured directly, and selected indicators are used for each. Health status, for example, is commonly approximated by age-specific mortality rates or incidence of selected diseases.

The indicators so defined derive their meaning solely from the context in which they are used. An infant mortality rate (deaths of infants under one year per 1,000 live births) is a statistic. It becomes an indicator by virtue of being chosen to describe a specific field. Indicators are normally numeral, but attempts to force concepts intrinsically unsuited to quantification into a numeric mould should be avoided.

The conceptual part of the work is clearly important (defining what is meant by development or health; then obtaining suitable indicators). The difficulties are greatly compounded in practice, particularly in some of the less-developed countries, by a scarcity of relevant data. In the present state of the art, the indicators actually selected often substitute only very imperfectly for reality, a fact to be remembered when considering conclusions of complex analysis involving the use of indicators.

Meanwhile, work on indicators proper (as distinct from social analysis, social reporting, programme evaluation, and so on) has tended to concentrate on three aspects: (1) to improve concepts and theory, for example through improved specification of the fields and more appropriate indicators; (2) to improve the supply of relevant data; and (3) to validate empirically selected indicators.

Other Definitions

Of the other definitions sometimes used in the literature none seems to distinguish indicators sufficiently from broader concepts, such as statistics. Thus, the term is occasionally employed in the sense of selecting a small number of key-variables (which are then called indicators) from a large number. However, deciding what is 'key' or crucial normally requires a theoretical framework involving the two-step procedure outlined above. The crucial elements are normally decided upon as part of the first step and not in the selection of indicators. Other criteria, for example that indicators be normative, that they be part of a model, or that they take the form of time series, although commonly features of indicators, have been criticized as unnecessarily restrictive.

The Meaning of 'Social'

There is no universally accepted meaning of 'social' indicators to distinguish them from economic or other kinds of indicators. The tendency has been to define social as a residual category to include everything that is not 'economic'. Commonly included fields are health, public safety, education, employment, income, housing, leisure, recreation, population as in the United States Bureau of the Census publication *Social Indicators*, to which in the UK's report *Social Trends* has been added: households and families, resources and expenditure, transport, communications and the environment, participation, social groups. Indicators of distribution, such as income distribution, are important. Researchers interested in structural change might add indicators of social differentiation or social organization; social psychologists could include indicators of social attitudes, and demographers indicators of population change.

Wolf Scott
United Nations Research Institute
for Social Development

Further Reading

Lard, K. C. (1983), 'Social indicators', *Annual Review of Sociology*, 9.

McGranahan, D. (1972), 'Development indicators and development models', *The Journal of Development Studies*, 8. (Special issue on development indicators, ed. N. Baster.)

Sheldon, E. B. and Moore, W. E. (eds) (1968), *Indicators of Social Change: Concepts and Measurements*, New York.

Social Welfare

The adjective 'economic' is perhaps more appropriate, since when it is discussed by economists, *'social' welfare* encompasses goods and services but not wider social issues. The modern approach is a fusion of two earlier approaches, a rough-and-ready 'statistical' approach and a finely-honed welfare analytic approach.

The statistical approach measures social welfare in terms of just two parameters: real income and its distribution. One's overall judgement is then to some degree subjective, depending upon how real income gains (or losses) are valued as against egalitarian losses (or gains). To capture the whole income distribution in one parameter is, of course, extremely arbitrary, but for many purposes (for example, cross-country comparisons) it is reasonably safe to take some measure of real income per head and an index of inequality like the Gini coefficient. The measurement of real income itself is not unambiguous because its composition changes over time as does its distribution. The composition aspect is intimately connected with both the theory of index numbers and the theory of consumer behaviour. To use current prices as weights for the different commodities is, however, a reasonable practical approximation to changes in real income. Distributional changes are more serious, and only in the rare case where real income had increased to the same degree for everyone could they be ignored. All this is essentially an elaboration of Pigou's double criterion that real income increase without the poor being worse off *or* that the poor be better off and real income not decrease.

It was thought for some time – by Kaldor and Hicks – that it would be desirable to use real income alone, without distributional judgements, to evaluate economic policies. This is because interpersonal comparisons were said to be 'unscientific'. The 'new welfare economics' advocated the use of a compensation principle: if adoption of a policy enabled the gainers to compensate the losers and still be better off, then the policy would bring an improvement. Later, due to Scitovsky, it had to be added that the losers could not then bribe the gainers to return to the original position. Controversy arose as to whether the principle was merely a test for real income increases or a criterion for improvement. Part of the difficulty lay in whether compensation was to be actual or merely hypothetical. In the 1950s, Little insisted, successfully, that distributional considerations would have to be reintroduced. Though the attempt to jettison distribution failed, there is still a feeling that real income is somehow more important and more fundamental, especially in the longer term (it is, after all, a *sine qua non*). The compensation principle was intended to be a test of economic efficiency from which it is not desirable to depart too far.

The other, welfare analytic, approach starts from the preferences of individuals rather than from aggregate income. Individual utilities are a function of individuals' goods and services, and social welfare is a function of individual utilities (Bergson, 1938). Together with competitive theory, this construction enables one to draw out certain optimality properties of markets – this is especially so if lump-sum redistributions (almost impossible in practice) are permitted. Most of these propositions, except those to do with redistribution, are independent of distributional weights and therefore robust against distributional preferences. Whatever these preferences, efficiency requires equality of marginal rates of substitution in production and consumption. So if lump-sum redistributions are possible, social welfare is maximized under competition with distribution being a separate 'political' matter. Unfortunately the dichotomy cannot be sustained, and there are no truly simple rules for maximizing social welfare.

A second use of the welfare analytic approach which has so far proved to be strongly negative (though usefully so) is relating social choice to individual preferences. There should, it was felt, be some method for moving from the latter to the former. Arrow (1951) showed that no such transition rule was possible. Starting from individual preference orderings, it is impossible to derive a social ordering without violating at least one of a number of perfectly reasonable axioms, for example, that the ordering be not imposed, not dictatorial, not restricted in domain, and so on. To give examples, a competitive mechanism has to be rejected because the domain is restricted to Pareto-improvements on the original allocation and a Bergsonian welfare function because it would have to be imposed (by an economist?). Social choice cannot therefore be grounded in individual preferences except for relatively trivial cases.

The modern reaction to these two weaknesses of the welfare analytic approach (the impossibility of lump-sum redistributions or of acceptable transition rules) is to be very much more explicit about distributional judgements and interpersonal comparisons. Failing that, work on social choice remains barren and formal. Following Atkinson (1970) a great deal of technical work has been done on the relationships between social-welfare functions and indices of inequality. There is scope within the approach for a whole spectrum of value judgements running from a zero preference for equality to Rawlsian emphasis on the income of the poorest. The modern approach moves away from Arrow's assumption that we have only ordinal information about individuals, without reverting to crude utilitarianism. In the same spirit it ventures to make statements about equivalence between individuals and to compare 'needs'. Social welfare can then be indexed (always provisionally) by statistical measures which certainly carry recognized value judgements with them but have good foundations in consumer theory. The measures are a compromise between statistical convenience and (possibly sterile) theoretical purity.

David Collard
University of Bath

References
Arrow, K. J. (1951), *Social Choice and Individual Values*, New York.
Atkinson, A. B. (1970), 'On the measurement of inequality', *Journal of Economic Theory*, 2.
Bergson, A. (1938), 'A reformulation of certain aspects of welfare economics', *Quarterly Journal of Economics*, 52.

Further Reading
Mishan, E. J. (1981), *Introduction to Normative Economics*, Oxford.
Sen, A. K. (1982), *Choice, Measurement and Welfare*, Oxford.
See also: *social welfare policy*.

Social Welfare Policy

In the long boom succeeding World War II, social welfare policy was widely seen as the state's intervention in society to secure the well-being of its citizens. This progressivist interpretation of increasing social expenditure by the state was sustained by the writings of key post-war welfare theorists such as Titmuss (1950) and Marshall (1967). The former welcomed increasing collectivism as a necessary and desirable means of enhancing social integration; the latter saw in the developing British Welfare State the extension of citizenship through the acquisition of social rights. The Beveridge-Keynes Welfare State, which had been called into existence by the exigencies of war and the balance of social forces in the post-war situation, came to assume an ideological significance, both as the exemplar against which other Welfare States were to be assessed, and also as an explanation of the development of the Welfare State itself. This ideological construction had few means of accounting for developments in other countries such as the pioneering achievements in social policy in New Zealand, nor of specifically conservative political strategies such as those of Bismarck's Germany, in which social insurance was conceived of as a mechanism to weaken the working-class movement and inhibit the spread of socialist ideas. For that matter, its emphasis on the peculiarly British nature of the achievement led to difficulties in explaining the rather better performance by most indicators of Britain's new partners when she joined the European Community, a phenomenon which was received with some shock by British political culture.

Relatively early on in the post-war period, social democratic theorists such as Crosland (1964) acknowledged the significance of social welfare policy and the achievement of the full employment economy in modifying a basically capitalist social formation. Nonetheless, redistribution was to be secured through growth, thus avoiding the political opposition of the rich – a strategy which was thrown into question as economic growth faltered and even declined. The significance of these policies for structuring sex-gender relations within the home and within the labour market was grasped very much more slowly (Wilson, 1977). Nonetheless, the achievement of the Welfare State or welfare capitalism, as it has been variously termed, was aided by the discourse and practices of social policy in which 'need' was set as morally and administratively superior to the market as the distributive principle for welfare. Thus integral to the achievement of welfare capitalism and institutional welfare was a concept of need which stood as an antagonistic value to that of capitalism with its, at best, residual welfare.

Need was at the same moment emancipatory and constrained within the dominant social relations. In its emancipatory aspect, need fostered the language of rights, not only in theoretical writing but within the popular demands of the new social movements which rose during the late 1960s and early 1970s within North America and Europe (Piven and Cloward, 1971; Rose, 1973). Aided by the 'rediscovery of poverty' in the 1960s (Harrington, 1962; Abel-Smith and Townsend, 1965), large-scale mobilization around income maintenance and housing exerted substantial pressure on governments to offer more, and more responsive, welfare provision. Thus, the new social movements shared with institutional welfare an opposition to mere residual welfare, but continuously sought to go beyond not only the level of existing provisions but also the organizational forms through which they were realized. Instead – and this tendency was to become magnified as the welfare movements were joined by the 1970s wave of feminism – existing forms of welfare were seen as coercive, inadequate and statist. In contrast, the oppositional forms developed by the movements themselves emphasized democratic accountability, and nonhierarchical ways of working. Freire's (1972) thesis of conscientization as the politically creative strategy for the poor in the Third World was shared by the new social movements as they sought to develop an alternative practice of welfare to what was usual in the old industrialized societies. At their most radical the new movements sought that society itself should be organized around the meeting of human need.

While the boom lasted, this critique of institutional welfare as statist and bureaucratic made relatively little impact on either mainstream social welfare policy thinking or on political culture: ideological support for a more or less institutional welfare overlaid the deeper antagonism between need and the market. The separation of need from market values was further facilitated by the separation between economic and social policy discourses. Social policy felt able to ignore economic policy since it was confident that Keynesian demand management techniques had delivered and would continue to deliver the precondition of the Welfare State, namely the full employment economy. Economists largely ignored the discussion of social welfare policy as of no interest to other than social ameliorists, until the crisis of the mid-1970s during which the loss of confidence in Keynesian techniques fostered a return to an endorsement of the market and an increasingly open opposition to state welfare expenditure (Friedman, 1962). Where institutional welfare had seen expanded welfare policies as socially integrative, a radical political economy had emphasized their contribution to capital accumulation and social control

(O'Connor, 1973; Gough, 1979); now monetarism and the advent of a new right saw such expenditures as harming individualism and competitiveness and thus weakening the central dynamic of capitalism. With considerable populist skill the new right acknowledged the critique of the coercive character of public welfare, and offered an increase in personal liberty through rolling back the (Welfare) State, restoring the market and the family as the paramount providers of welfare.

The very depth of the current crisis which has provided the conditions for the rise of the new right, nonetheless serves as a major constraint for its remedies. Global restructuring of manufacturing is associated with widespread and foreseeably long-term unemployment in the de-industrializing countries. Unemployment, averaging around 12 per cent in the OECD countries in 1982 and with few clear indications of a significant improvement, requires, even in the most residual conception of welfare, substantial expenditure for both maintenance and control of an expanding surplus population. This situation is aggravated by the large numbers of young people among the unemployed, among whom ethnic and racial minorities are over-represented.

Despite these political constraints, since 1975 most Western governments have reduced the rate of growth of their social welfare budgets. Thus, up to 1975 the real rate of social expenditure growth in the seven largest OECD countries was no less than 8 per cent per annum (15 per cent growth at current prices); between 1975 and 1981 the real rate was halved. While all countries have experienced difficulties in maintaining their social welfare budget in the face of the reduction of the growth of the overall economy, governments with a specifically anti-welfare ideology such as the US and Britain have made substantial inroads. Thus, in the case of Britain an institutional system of welfare moves increasingly towards a residual model, particularly in the area of social security. The Nordic countries stand apart as the last bastion of the most highly developed expression of the old Welfare State, although the mix of labour market and social policies through which they achieve this varies substantially between them. Given the double significance for women of the existence of the Welfare State, as potential provider of both employment and services, it is perhaps not by chance that those Nordic countries with a continuing commitment to welfare have also an unusually high proportion of women representatives in their parliaments and upper houses. It is noteworthy that writers from these countries, such as Himmelstrand (1981) and his co-workers, are taking an active part in the current international debate concerning the possible future direction open to a post-Welfare State society. These writers seek to develop a theory which looks beyond welfare capitalism, to a new but very much more democratically based corporatism. Such post-Welfare State theorists are typically not unsympathetic to the claims of the new social movements (Gorz, 1982). However, they seem not to have fully appreciated the significance of feminist theorizing concerning the relationship between paid and unpaid labour within the development of the Welfare State, and thus the advantage to the dominant gender of retaining the present arrangements. Thus, even though the precondition of the old Welfare State, the full employment of one gender with welfare flowing through the man to the dependent family, no longer fits the actuality of either domestic or labour market structures, the ideological defence of those arrangements persists. Faced with the growing 'feminization of poverty' (Pearce, 1978), and the profoundly segregated (by both occupation and between full and part-time employment) labour market, there is a serious question concerning the extent to which the needs of women are met by the new post-Welfare State theorizing.

These are cautious, even sceptical reflections on the debate around the Welfare State and the place of social welfare policy (Glennister, 1983). How far any of the new theories can offer to serve as the new fusion of the social and the economic, the contemporary historical equivalent of the old Welfare State of Keynes and Beveridge is not yet clear. What is clear, however, is that social welfare policy having spent its years of greatest growth relatively detached from economic policy has now been forcibly rejoined by circumstance. Together they occupy the centre of an intensely debated political arena.

Hilary Rose
University of Bradford

References
Abel-Smith, B. and Townsend, P. (1965), *The Poor and the Poorest*, London.
Crosland, C. A. R. (1964), *The Future of Socialism*, London.
Freire, P. (1972), *Cultural Action for Freedom*, Harmondsworth.
Friedman, M. (1962), *Capitalism and Freedom*, Chicago.
Glennister, H. (ed.) (1983), *The Future of the Welfare State*, London.
Gorz, A. (1982), *Farewell to the Working Class*, London.
Gough, I. (1979), *The Political Economy of Welfare*, London.
Harrington, M. (1962), *The Other America*, Harmondsworth.
Himmelstrand, U., Ahrne, G., Lundberg, L. and Lundberg, L. (1981), *Beyond Welfare Capitalism; Issues Actors and Social Forces in Societal Change*, London.
Marshall, T. H. (1967), *Social Policy*, 2nd edn, London.
O'Connor, J. (1973), *The Fiscal Crisis of the State*, New York.
Pearce, D. (1978), 'The feminization of poverty: women, work and welfare', *Urban and Social Change Review*.
Piven, F. F. and Cloward, R. (1971), *Regulating the Poor: The Functions of Public Welfare*, New York.
Rose, H. (1973), 'Up against the Welfare State: the claimant unions', in R. Miliband and J. Saville (eds), *The Socialist Register*, London.
Titmuss, R. M. (1950), *Problems of Social Policy*, London.
Wilson, E. (1977), *Women and the Welfare State*, London.
See also: *social welfare; social work*.

Social Work

It is perhaps not surprising that the term social work, combining the rich ambiguity of 'social' with the misleading and somewhat deterrent simplicity of 'work', has undergone considerable change in usage since it first appeared in England

towards the end of the last century. It was then used to describe
a perspective applicable from a number of different occupations
rather than to announce the arrival of a particular new occupation. This perspective derived from the serious reconsider-
ation of the role of citizen, and it can be illustrated from the
dedication of a book entitled *The Spirit of Social Work* (Devine,
1911) to 'social workers, that is to say, to every man and
woman, who, in any relation of life, professional, industrial,
political, educational or domestic; whether on salary or as a
volunteer; whether on his own individual account or as part of
an organized movement, is working consciously, according to
his light intelligently and according to his strength persistently,
for the promotion of the common welfare'. (The fact that Devine
was an American, indicates the speed with which 'social work'
was exported to America and thence, eventually, to many other
societies, developed and developing.)

This broadly brushed backcloth has been more or less evident
in the present century as social workers have attempted to claim
a role that is specialized and professional. It is perhaps one
reason why an agreed and satisfactory definition of 'social work'
is not yet forthcoming. Other features of social work activity
have also contributed to this lack of agreement about the nature
of social work. The broad purposes of social work have become
more ambiguous as social workers have increasingly become
state employees rather than volunteers or paid workers in non-
statutory agencies. Sometimes public appreciation of social
work has been blunted by the large claims made on behalf
of social workers (for instance, that social work can cure a
considerable range of private sorrows and public ills or simply
that social workers represent the conscience of society). Changes
in the dominant theories said to underpin social work – economics or sociology or psychoanalytic theories – and confusion
between espoused theories and those actually informing practice
have created at least the impression of significant ruptures as
a tradition of practice struggles to assert itself. Finally, social
work, like teaching, is both an 'attempting' and a 'succeeding'
term: on occasions practitioners will deny the term to activity

that was not particularly successful or that infringed one of the contested maxims that figure largely in professional talk.

A rough description of the contemporary social worker is of a person (traditionally a woman but increasingly in some societies a man) who as a representative of some statutory or non-statutory agency delivers a wide range of services, from income maintenance and welfare commodities, to directive and non-directive counselling. These services are directed or offered to individuals or to groups of different kinds, based on kinship, locality, interest or common condition. For the efficient and effective delivery of such services, social workers claim to use skills of various kinds, a range of theoretical and practical knowledge, and a set of values specific to social work.

Definition or general description take us some way towards grasping social work, but a more productive approach is to examine certain key questions concerning the form and the purposes of social work that have arisen at different times in the present century. In relation to form, two questions predominate: is social work to be treated as a profession (and if so, what kind of profession); is social work to be practised as an applied science, as an art, or as some kind of ministration? Flexner's (1915) consideration of the professional nature of social work raised questions that may still fruitfully be pursued. He concluded that social work met some of the criteria for professional status, but that social workers were mediators rather than full professional agents, that they pursued no distinctive ends, and that they were required to possess certain personal qualities rather than expertise in scientifically-derived technical skills. More recently, it has been suggested that social work can most easily be viewed as a semi-profession or as a bureau-profession. The characterization of social work as part of a humanistic as contrasted with a scientific movement is best studied through the work of Halmos (1965).

Controversy within social work is somewhat rare, but important questioning concerning the purpose of social work can be appreciated through three major debates (Timms, 1983). The first, between leaders of the influential Charity Organiz-ation Society and the Socialists at the turn of the century, concerned the emphasis to be given to the individual and to his social circumstances and to preventive as opposed to curative work. The second, between two American schools of social work, the Functionalists and the Diagnosticians in the middle of the century, raised questions concerning the independence of social work as a helping process contrasted with a process of psychological treatment. The third, most immediate, controversy revolves around the possibility of a social work that is politically radical or, specifically, Marxist.

Noel Timms
University of Leicester

References

Devine, E. (1911), *The Spirit of Social Work*, New York.
Flexner, A. (1915), 'Is social work a profession?', *Proceedings of the 42nd National Conference of Charities and Correction*.
Halmos, P. (1965), *The Faith of the Counsellors*, London.
Timms, N. (1983), *Social Work Values: An Enquiry*, London.

Further Reading

Younghusband, E. (1978), *Social Work in Britain: 1950–1975*, 2 vols, London.
Timms, N. and Timms, R. (1982), *Dictionary of Social Welfare*, London.
See also: *social welfare policy*.

Stress

The breadth of the topic of stress is reflected both in the diversity of fields of research with which it is associated and in the difficulty of finding an adequate definition. Some stresses such as noise, heat or pain might best be considered as properties of the environment which represent departure from optimum and which differ only in intensity from levels which are normally tolerable. Thus, stress could be seen as a stimulus characteristic, perhaps best defined as an 'intense level of everyday life'. In contrast, it is possible to envisage stress as a pattern of responses associated with autonomic arousal. Initial impetus for this approach was provided by Selye (1956), who proposed that stress is the nonspecific response of the body to any demand made upon it. Physiologically committed, it assumed that the stress response was not influenced by the nature of the stressful event, but was part of a universal pattern of defence termed the 'General Adaptation Syndrome'. Selye demonstrated a temporal pattern in cases of prolonged stress. There were three identifiable phases: alarm, resistance and exhaustion. The capacity of the organism to survive was assumed to be a function of exposure time; resistance to further stress was lowered in the alarm phase, raised in the subsequent resistance phase and further lowered in the exhaustion phase.

Neither stimulus-based nor response-based definitions cope well with varied and complex stresses such as taking an examination, parachute jumping, surgical operations and public speaking. The problem that 'one man's stress is another man's challenge' is partly solved by a definition which presupposes that stress is the result of imbalance between demand and capacity, and, more importantly, by the *perception* that there is imbalance. The factors which create ambition and translate into intentions are as important in determining stress levels as those which affect capacity.

A number of models have been proposed which assume that the conditions for stress are met when demands tax or exceed adjustive resources (Lazarus, 1966, 1976; Cox and Mackay, 1978). In particular, Lazarus has proposed that several appraisal processes are involved in the assessment of threat. The intensity of threat depends on stimulus features, but also on the perceived ability to cope. In turn, coping may take the form of direct action or avoidance and may involve anticipatory preparation against harm, or the use of cognitive defence strategies.

Fisher (1984) has proposed that mental activity in the perception and response to stress forms the essential basis of worry and preoccupation, and is likely to be concerned with the assessment and establishment of control. The perception of personal control is not only a likely determinant of psychological response, but has been shown to determine hormone pattern.

For example, applied and laboratory studies have suggested that control over the work pace dictates the pattern of noradrenaline and adrenaline balance, and may determine the degree of experienced anxiety.

Working conditions and events in life history together form an important source of potential stress and may have a pervasive influence on mental state and physical health in the long term. Stress at work is no longer thought to be the prerogative of white-collar and professional workers. Repetitive manual work is associated with high adrenaline levels; paced assembly line workers have been found to be very anxious, and computer operators who spend more than 90 per cent of their time working at the interface may be tense for 'unwind periods' after work. Depression is likely when personal discretion is reduced, when there is lack of social support, or when social communication is impaired, as in conditions of high machine noise.

A significant additional feature of life history is the adjustment required by change. Two important consequences of change are interruption of previously established activity and the introduction of uncertainty about future control. Studies of homesickness in university students have suggested the importance of worry and preoccupation as features of adjustment to change. Grieving for the previous life style is as much a feature as concern about the new, and in some individuals this may be an important prerequisite for the establishment of control (Fisher, 1984; Fisher *et al.*, 1985).

Competence is a necessary condition of the exercise of personal control, but it may be difficult to maintain in stressful circumstance. Studies of the effects of environmental stress on attention and memory have indicated changes in function in relatively mild conditions of stress. Although the changes may not always be detrimental in mildly stressful conditions, at high levels of stress, behavioural disorganization and consequent loss of control are characteristic. It has been found that performance is related to arousal level in the form of an inverted 'U' curve. Mild stresses, by increasing arousal, are likely to improve performance, whereas severe stresses are more likely to cause deterioration. However, the assumption of a single dimension of arousal has been undermined by physiological evidence suggesting that there are arousal patterns which may be stimulus or response specific. The concept of compatibility between concurrent and stress-produced arousal levels is proposed by Fisher (1984) as part of a composite model of the relationship between stress and performance. The model also takes into account the influence of worry and mental preoccupation associated with stress and the establishment of control as joint determinants of performance change.

In both occupational and life-stress conditions, the pattern of behaviour – and hence the accompanying hormone balance which features in a particular stress problem – may result from decision making about control. A critical decision concerns whether a person is helpless or able to exercise control. The mental processes involved in control assessment may involve detecting and summarizing the relationship between actions and consequences over a period of time. In dogs, prior treatment by inescapable shock was shown to produce inappropriate helplessness in later avoidance learning (Seligman, 1975), which led to the hypothesis that depression and helplessness are closely associated, and may be transmitted as expectancies about loss of control. The question 'Why are we not all helpless?' is appropriate, given the high probability that most people experience helplessness on occasions in their lives. It has been partly answered by research which suggests that normal subjects resist helplessness and depression by overestimating control when rewards are forthcoming (Alloy and Abramson, 1979). Equally, they may put more effort into a task, or find other evidence suggesting that control is possible, thus raising self-esteem (Fisher, 1984). By contrast, those already depressed assess control levels accurately, but are more likely to blame themselves for circumstances which indicate that there is no control. Therefore, lack of optimistic bias and lack of objectivity in attributing the cause of failure distinguishes the depressed from the non-depressed person.

The above considerations suggest that analysis of decisions about control in different stressful circumstances may provide the key to understanding the risks attached to long-term health changes in an individual. A person who is too readily helpless may be depressed and may incur the punishment produced by control failure. He thus experiences distress. A person who struggles against the odds of success incurs the penalty of high effort. A person who practises control by avoidance may need to be constantly vigilant, and to evolve elaborate techniques for avoidance and, if successful, will never receive the information which indicates control is effective.

The outcome of decision making about control could have implications for physical health because of the mediating role of stress hormones. Repeated high levels of catecholamines may, because of functional abuse of physical systems, increase the risk of chronic illness such as heart disease. High levels of corticoid hormones may change the levels of antibody response, thus changing the risk associated with virus and bacterial born illness, as well as diseases such as cancer (Totman, 1979; Cox and Mackay, 1982).

S. Fisher
University of Dundee

References

Alloy, L. B. and Abramson, L. Y. (1979), 'Judgements of contingency in depressed or non-depressed students: sadder but wiser?', *Journal of Experimental Psychology (General)*, 108.

Cox, T. and Mackay, C. (1982), 'Psychosocial factors and psychophysiological mechanisms in the aetiology and development of cancers', *Society of Science and Medicine*, 16.

Fisher, S. A. (1984), *Stress and the Perception of Control*, Hillsdale, NJ.

Fisher, S., Murray, K. and Frazer, N. (1985), 'Homesickness, health and efficiency in first year students', *Journal of Environmental Psychology*, 5.

Lazarus, R. (1966), *Psychological Stress and the Coping Process*, New York.

Lazarus, R. (1976), *Patterns of Adjustment*, Tokyo.

Seligman, M. E. P. (1975), *Helplessness: On Depression Development and Death*, San Francisco.
Selye, H. (1956), *The Stress of Life*, New York.
Totman, R. (1979), *The Social Causes of Illness*, London.
See also: *bereavement*.

Subculture

In common parlance the term, subculture, is used most often to describe those special worlds of interest and identification that set apart some individuals, groups, and/or larger aggregations from the larger societies to which they belong. We speak of youth subcultures, ethnic subcultures, regional subcultures, occupational subcultures, and the subcultures which develop among those who share special interests such as stamp collecting, bird watching, or drug use.

Yet neither membership in a particular category (race, ethnicity, age, sex, occupation, or area of residence) nor behaviour (drug abuse or bird watching) is sufficient to account for or to characterize a subculture. The critical element, rather, is the degree to which values, artifacts, and identification are shared among and with other members of a category, or those who engage in a particular type of behaviour. Such sharing is enhanced by the extent of *social separation* between members of the larger society and those who belong to a particular category, or those who engage in particular behaviours. Hair colour, for example, is prominent in descriptions of individuals, but is not a basis for social separation. The social structural characteristics noted above, and many types of behaviour, have become major bases for social separation.

Subcultures exist in relation to larger cultures and societies. The nature of these relationships is critical to the origin, development, and the status of subcultures within societies. They may be merely different, and be viewed indifferently; they may be viewed positively; or, because defined as deviant, viewed negatively. Some are not merely different, but oppositional to major cultural values, in which case they are properly termed contra- or countercultures. Definitions and experiences involving subcultural 'outsiders' and 'insiders', as well as *among* 'insiders', exert powerful, often determining, influences on subcultures. Suspicion, distrust, and fear of the different, deviant, and/or unknown, may lead to rejection by the dominant society, particularly when those who are so defined also lack power. A cycle of interaction may thus be set in motion in which those who are defined as different, and so on, are increasingly thrown on their own resources, develop their own values, beliefs, roles and status systems. Examples are delinquent and lower-class subcultures, religious sects and other groups which withdraw from the larger society. Conversely, powerful groups are able to command the resources necessary to avoid many of the negative effects, if not always the negative definitions, of their difference. 'High society', the professions, and learned disciplines come immediately to mind. As these examples suggest, organizational forms and subcultures should not be confused, though they are mutually reinforcing.

Structural differentiation of societies provides the boundary conditions for subcultural formation. Changes in structural differentiation produce subcultural changes. Subcultures thus are inevitably linked to social change, serving both as the 'engines' of social change and as resisters to it. For example, the esoteric knowledge, language, and techniques of science promote the discovery of further knowledge and its application; but the vested interests in occupations and professions – and identification with the past which is often associated with subcultures – resist change.

Subcultures vary along many dimensions: rigidity of separation, degree of exclusivity, how much of the lives of participating individuals is encompassed, the extent to which they are group centred or more diffuse among those who identify or are identified with them, and the extent to which they overlap with other subcultures. Numerous theories have attempted to account for these and other characteristics and variations of subcultures, but no general theory of subcultures has been entirely successful.

James F. Short Jr
Washington State University

Further Reading

Cohen, S. (1980), *Folk Devils and Moral Panics*, 2nd edn, New York.

Cressey, D. R. (1983), 'Delinquent and criminal subcultures', in S. E. Kadish (ed.), *Encyclopaedia of Crime and Justice*, New York.

Fischer, C. S. (1982), *To Dwell Among Friends: Personal Networks in Town and City*, Chicago.

Yinger, J. M. (1960), 'Contraculture and subculture', *American Sociological Review*, 25.

Yinger, J. M. (1977), 'Presidential address: countercultures and social change', *American Sociological Review*, 42.

See also: *gangs*.

Suicide

Social science research into the causes of suicide can be classified into five major explanatory categories: early childhood experiences and personality; cultural factors; social integration; economic conditions, and modernization.

(1) Suicide in adulthood has been linked to experiences in the family of origin and to certain character traits: loss of a parent, chronic love withdrawal, being a first-born child, and the suicidal behaviour of relatives (Lester, 1972). Personality characteristics often associated with suicide include depression, impulsiveness, pessimism, negative self-concept, passivity, introversion and dichotomous thinking. Psychologists tend to link these traits with early childhood trauma, while sociologists are more likely to associate them with events in adulthood, including divorce and unemployment.

(2) The cultural explanations of suicide stress values, cultural-role expectations, and the influence of the media. For example, male role expectations in Western society have been associated with suicide – males are expected to be 'strong', therefore they are less able than females to cope with crises. But given the recent convergence in sex roles, the differences between rates of suicide in the sexes are decreasing in most industrial nations. American studies have also found that there are cultural differ-

ences in the manner in which members of the different racial groups internalize aggression; again, with the decline of racial separation and discrimination in the US, these differences are less marked than before, and consequently suicide rates are similar in the different racial groups (Stack, 1982). Finally, in the US and Britain, suicide stories carried in the media have been found to increase slightly the suicide rate (Phillips, 1974).

(3) Suicide research continues to investigate social integration, or the degree of subordination of the individual's self-interest to the group. Its components include marital, religious and political dimensions. Researchers have found that the higher the marital integration (low divorce rate) of a group, the lower its suicide rate (Stack, 1982). However, earlier findings that Catholics had a lower suicide rate than Protestants have not been supported by recent research. Other measures of religiosity, for example, church attendance, have been shown to reduce the likelihood of suicide. Durkheim's contention that political crises such as war decrease suicide by rousing collective sentiments has recently also been seriously questioned (Stack, 1982). Multivariate research in the US indicates that it is full employment during wartime, rather than aroused collective sentiments, that is responsible for the lower suicide rates (Marshall, 1981). Migration too is positively associated with suicide. This is because migrants have to renounce close ties with friends, family and co-workers (Stack, 1980).

(4) Economically-deprived groups and the unemployed have higher suicide rates, while improvements in economic conditions appear to reduce the rate. The world-wide trend towards a lower suicide rate among elderly males has been attributed to better social security programmes.

(5) Durkheim also attributed the increase of suicide in the nineteenth century to the process of modernization. Factors such as the rise of individualism, urbanization, industrialization, and the replacement of religious authority with free inquiry in the educational system, were seen as lowering social integration. But present-day research does not find a relation-

ship between modernization and suicide. While in some nations suicide has increased, in others it has decreased or levelled off. Other factors, for example, commitment to education, have been suggested as explanations.

There has been a most striking post-war surge in suicide in industrial nations among young people aged between fifteen and twenty-four. Some of the reasons for this are: massive unemployment and its associated frustrations, even among highly educated people; the decline of religious identification; increased tolerance of deviant behaviour in the youth subculture; and the emotional consequences of divorce on children (Waldron and Eyer, 1975; Stack, 1983).

Steven Stack
Pennsylvania State University

References

Durkheim, E. (1951 [1897]), *Suicide – A Sociological Study*, London. (Original French edn, *Le Suicide: étude sociologique*, Paris.)

Lester, D. (1972), *Why People Kill Themselves: A 1980's Summary of Research Findings on Suicidal Behavior*, Springfield, Ill.

Marshall, J. (1981), 'Political integration and the effect of war on suicide', *Social Forces*, 59.

Phillips, D. (1974), 'The influence of suggestion on suicide', *American Sociological Review*, 59.

Stack, S. (1980), 'Interstate migration and the rate of suicide', *International Journal of Social Psychiatry*, 26.

Stack, S. (1982), 'Suicide: a decade review of the sociological literature', *Deviant Behavior*, 4.

Stack, S. (1983), 'The effect of the decline in institutionalized religion on suicide, 1954–1978', *Journal for the Scientific Study of Religion*, 22.

Waldron, I. and Eyer, J. (1975), 'Socioeconomic causes of the recent rise in death rates for 15–24 year olds', *Social Science and Medicine*, 9.

Work and Leisure

Work can refer to any physical and/or mental activities which transform natural materials into a more useful form, improve human knowledge and understanding of the world, and/or provide or distribute goods to others. The definition of work cannot be limited to references to activities alone, however, but most also consider the purposes for which, and the social context within which, those activities are being carried out. For some people, their 'work' is to play games to entertain spectators, games such as football, tennis or snooker which many others play for their own pleasure and relaxation; to read a book for interest or amusement has a different significance from reading the same book in order to prepare a lecture. Work activities are instrumental activities: they are undertaken in order to meet certain individual needs either directly, or indirectly by providing for the needs of others so that goods and services, or the means to purchase them, are received in exchange. Work activities may also be valued for their own sake, but they always have an extrinsic purpose.

In industrial societies the most socially prominent and economically important forms of work are those activities which occur within relationships of employment, or self-employment, and provide goods and services for sale in the market in return for a wage, salary or fee. This predominance of one social context and form of organization of work is a relatively recent development; within human history as a whole the direct provision of a family's or a community's needs (as in peasant societies), or production carried out under coercion (for example serfdom, or slavery), have been much more common. Indeed the development of industrial societies necessitated not only considerable social innovation in forms of work organization (such as factories and offices) but also the emergence and internalization of new values regarding work, ones which provided the necessary sense of obligation to work hard and in a rational and regular way under the control of others (Thompson, 1967). Such a 'work ethic', whose origins were seen by Weber (1930 [1922]) as lying particularly in certain forms of Protestantism, has however coexisted with the more traditional view of work as a necessity. Whereas when work is viewed as a moral duty, of value in itself, not to work is to be 'idle'; when work is a tiresome necessity, not to work is to have 'leisure'.

The current importance of work within an employment relationship and a market context should not obscure those forms of work which are differently structured and located. Of particular importance is domestic work, which is often very time consuming and clearly makes a considerable and absolutely essential contribution to the economy, though one which is only rarely acknowledged. Also part of the so-called 'informal' economy are other household activities such as do-it-yourself home improvements and exchanges of help and services between relatives and neighbours; activities in the wider community such as voluntary work; and work in the 'hidden economy': jobs 'on the side' for pay which is not taxed, and the clearly illegal 'work' of criminals (Gershuny and Pahl, 1980).

Leisure

A definition of leisure is equally difficult. It can be used to refer to a quality of life (leisure as the mark of a 'gentleman'), or to refer to some combination of time, activity and experience: time free from work and other necessary activities such as eating and sleeping; 'play' activities which are outside normal routines; and experiences which are intrinsically rewarding (Roberts, 1981; Parker, 1971). Whilst leisure can fairly clearly be distinguished from paid employment, it may be much more difficult to separate it from other forms of work such as housework or voluntary work. Leisure is also differently experienced and unevenly available: people with jobs (especially men) have more clearly demarcated leisure time and activities than those with domestic responsibilities, such as housewives, whose 'work is never done'.

During recent years a major preoccupation has been with unemployment, the lack of paid work for all those able and willing to do it. In so far as current levels of unemployment are seen as due to structural changes in the economies of industrial societies, and especially the use of mini-computers, robots and so on to replace human labour, they have raised the question of whether we may be seeing the start of a 'leisure society', one in which it will no longer be normal for all adults to work, and where there will be far more leisure and maybe even the need to 'work' at one's leisure activities (Jenkins and Sherman, 1979, 1981). There are, of course, a lot of unresolved questions about such a future for work and leisure: (1) It is far from clear that the potential of the new technology is as great as has been claimed, and if it is, whether that potential can be realized in ways which will release people from employment. (2) There are considerable problems in ensuring that the economic benefits of the new technology are distributed in ways which reward people generally rather than just the few: existing fiscal and tax arrangements are certainly far from adequate. (3) Even if many people can be provided with a high standard of living without the need to undertake (much) paid employment, there is a motivational problem: who is going to be prepared to do the remaining heavy, repetitive, unpleasant or unrewarding jobs once pay is no longer an incentive?

Most important of all, we need to consider the social and psychological functions currently filled by work, and especially paid employment, and to ask whether leisure, even if it is 'worked at', or any other activities, can provide alternatives. Can leisure structure the day as work and employment do; provide social contacts outside the immediate family and locality; link individuals to goals and purposes outside themselves; give a sense of identity and status; and enforce activity and through that some sense of control over events (Jahoda, 1982)? Work provides a sense of necessity and constrains what we can do; for this reason it is often resented and contrasted unfavourably with leisure and 'free time'; paradoxically without the constraint the sense of freedom may also be lost.

Richard K. Brown
University of Durham

References

Gershuny, J. I. and Pahl, R. E. (1980), 'Britain in the decade of the three economies', *New Society*, 3.

Jahoda, M. (1982), *Employment and Unemployment*, Cambridge.

Jenkins, C. and Sherman, B. (1979), *The Collapse of Work*, London.

Jenkins, C. and Sherman, B. (1981), *The Leisure Shock*, London.

Parker, S. R. (1971), *The Future of Work and Leisure*, London.

Roberts, K. (1981), *Leisure*, London.

Thompson, E. P. (1967), 'Time, work discipline and industrial capitalism', *Past and Present*, 38.

Weber, M. (1930 [1922]) *The Protestant Ethic and the Spirit of Capitalism*, London. (Original German edn, *Die protestantische Ethik und der 'Geist' des Kapitalismus*, Tübingen.)

Further reading

Abrams, P. and Brown, R. K. (eds) (1984), *UK Society: Work, Urbanism and Inequality*, London.

Anthony, P. D. (1977), *The Ideology of Work*, London.

Esland, G. and Salaman, G. (1980), *The Politics of Work and Occupations*, Milton Keynes.

Gershuny, J. (1978), *After Industrial Society*, London.

Hedges, N. and Beynon, H. (1982), *Born to Work*, London.